Enjoying Music

Whether you're tone-deaf or able to tell if it's Karajan or Davis conducting with your eyes closed, this book will enable you to get more out of music. It will increase your knowledge of the history and technicalities of music as well as the whole range of orchestral instruments, composers – from Henry Purcell to Andrew Lloyd Webber – musical forms, and even tell you where to hear music live.

Jean Richardson is an author and journalist who has written two other Beaver Books, *Enjoying Ballet* and *The Beaver Book of the Seaside.*

Enjoying Music

Jean Richardson

Illustrated by Clive Spong

Beaver Books

First published in 1979 by
The Hamlyn Publishing Group Limited
London · New York · Sydney · Toronto
Astronaut House, Feltham, Middlesex, England

ISBN 0 600 36353 8

Set, printed and bound in England by
Cox and Wyman Limited, Reading
Set in Linotype Pilgrim

Acknowledgements

The photographs in this book were supplied by the following: Reg Wilson – Plate 1; Camera Press Ltd – Plates 2 (Karsh of Ottowa) and 12; Keystone Press Agency – Plates 3, 4 and 5; BBC – Plates 6, 10 and 11; Appollo Photography – Plate 7; Genista Streeten Publicity (Zöe Dominic) Plates 8 and 9.

Part of the score of Benjamin Britten's *The Young Person's Guide to the Orchestra* on page 97 is reprinted by permission of Boosey and Hawkes Music Publishers Ltd. © Copyright 1947 by Hawkes & Son (London) Ltd.

The diagrams on pages 28 and 88 are taken from *Introducing Music* (Pelican Books, 1965) by Ottó Károlyi, © Ottó Károlyi 1965, and are reprinted by permission of Penguin Books Ltd.

The author and publishers would also like to thank the following for information about children's concerts: Children's Concert Centre; East Midlands Arts; Hallé Concerts Society; Scottish Arts Council; Scottish Chamber Orchestra; Scottish National Orchestra Society; Scottish Opera; Welsh Arts Council; Yorkshire Arts Association; Youth & Music.

Contents

1 Learning to listen

When most people talk about learning music they mean learning to play an instrument so that you can make music yourself. Certainly if you do get the chance you should seize it, but lots of people who love music and get a great deal of pleasure out of it, don't have the opportunity or the time to do more than listen. Yet listening isn't as easy as it sounds, and although anyone can listen to music without any special training, there are different kinds of listening, and you really do get more out of music if you know something about it.

This then is a book for listeners rather than performers. It doesn't take for granted that you know anything about music, but it does see you as someone who feels you would like music even more and understand it better if you had some kind of musical background, some introduction to the music going on around you, on the radio and television, on records, and best of all, live in concert halls.

There are many different ways of approaching music – through its history, through the lives of the great composers, through the various musical forms such as symphonies and concertos – but I find that when I go to a concert the first thing I am aware of are the musicians and their instruments. The shapes themselves are intriguing. Why do some instruments seem to need miles of tubing while others are quite short? How do you tell the difference between an oboe and a clarinet? Is it very difficult to play those tempting drums? And when the conductor comes on, I am fascinated by his part. Why is he famous? Does he really need to make such wild gestures and sing to the orchestra?

I am, as you can see, caught up in the actual performance of the music. I may know the work I'm going to hear very well – perhaps I've got a record of it – but when I hear it live and can connect the sounds I hear with the players in front of me, I become aware of the music in a more vital way. So if much of your listening is done at home, it's even more important to be aware of the orchestra as a group of instruments which each has its own history, sound, and distinctive qualities.

The music and instruments that we hear today are the result of a response to sound that began thousands of years ago. Various noises appealed particularly to primitive man's imagination – just as they do to ours – and he responded first to a regular beat or rhythm, and then to sounds that joined together to make a recognisable shape or tune.

Few of the actual instruments used by early man have survived, but we have some idea what they were like from the primitive instruments still played in many parts of the world such as Central and South America, the Pacific, and Africa.

The first instruments were not used for music-making as we know it, but for ritualistic purposes. From the beginning, man was aware that his survival depended on forces outside his control. No matter how hard he worked on the land, he needed rain and warmth to make the grain sprout and ripen. No matter how bold a hunter or how brave a fighter he was, he needed a measure of luck to help him capture his prey or defeat his enemies.

So in order to get fate on his side, he took part in ceremonies that were designed to please whatever gods he believed in.

Such ceremonies often involved dancing, and the dancers needed a definite rhythm with a clear, stressed beat. At first they provided this by clapping, but then they realised that something that could be shaken or clashed together would be even more effective. They tended to use whatever was nearest to hand. Rattles were made of anything that could be filled with dried seeds or pebbles, or strung together, such as pieces of wood and bone. Clappers were made of wood, ivory, and, much later, metal, and they were sometimes shaped to represent a pair of hands.

Man used the earth itself as an instrument. He stamped on it with his feet, or dug a hole and laid some pieces of wood across it. When he struck the wood, the hole helped to make the sound louder, and this was the origin of the xylophone, which is used today in school percussion bands and in symphony orchestras. Other early instruments very like this were pieces of stone that were struck with a heavy beater, and pieces of metal that were the forerunners of the modern glockenspiel.

Many primitive instruments were probably first discovered by accident, and this kind of 'accident' still happens today. The steel drum that appears in the very popular Caribbean steel bands was invented in Trinidad during the Second World War. It started out as an ordinary oil drum, but some rhythm-happy drummer got going on it and saw how to turn it into a lively instrument capable of producing a variety of notes.

The drum was a very popular early instrument. It was believed to have the power to summon thunder (the thunder god was worshipped in many areas) and to chase away evil spirits, and it was also good at frightening the enemy. Later on, armies were to recognise its usefulness,

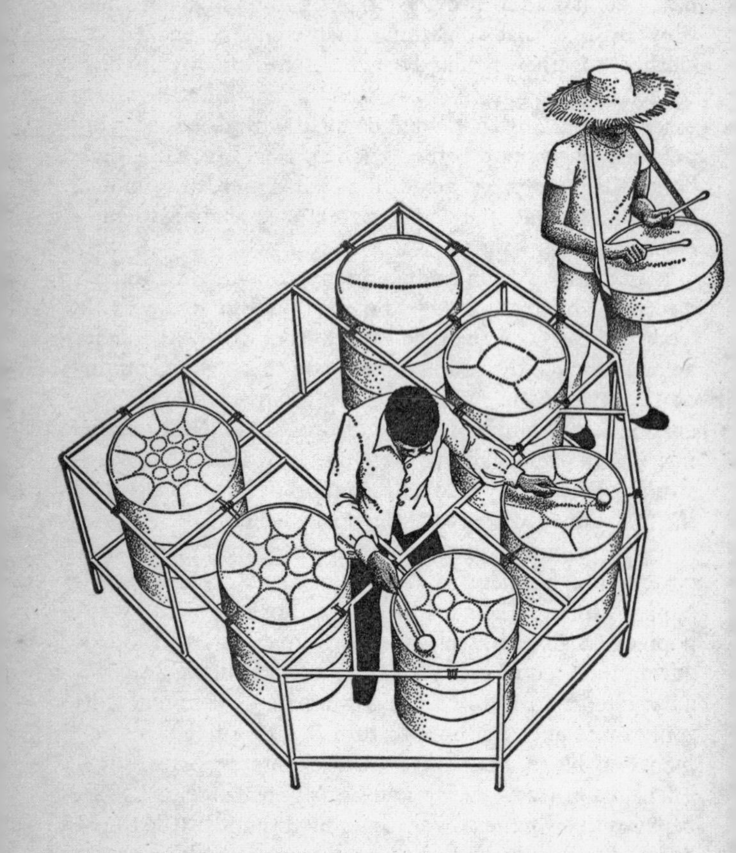

A West Indian steel band

and while the fife (a kind of flute) played a tune, the drum would beat out a regular rhythm for the soldiers to march to.

It was probably by chance that man discovered that striking or plucking strings of different lengths produced different notes. One of the first stringed instruments was simply a hole in the ground with a piece of string stretched over it. The principle on which it worked was not unlike that of the violin, which wasn't invented until thousands of years later. The hunter's bow was also used as an instrument, and the string was made to vibrate by tapping it with a stick or plucking it with the fingers. In time, it was bowed with a second bow. Man also discovered how to vary the notes by making the string longer or shorter, and you can find out how and why this worked on page 35.

Similarly man found that he could make a pleasing noise by blowing across the end of a tube, and that the note was higher or lower according to the length of the pipe. It could also be changed by making holes in the pipe, and if you've had the chance to play the recorder, you'll know how these finger-holes work.

Early flutes were often made of the bones of animals, and were thought to have a special hunting magic. The way in which they could attract animals is celebrated in the famous story of the Pied Piper of Hamelin. He, you may remember, called forth all the rats who were plaguing the town of Hamelin, and then when the town councillors refused to pay him a proper reward, he went on playing and lured away all the children too.

Man also discovered how to play pipes by putting a reed inside them that vibrated when he blew, and how to blow the horns and tusks of animals, and later on he imitated these natural forms in metal. The early uses of such instruments were often connected with religion, warfare, and magic. According to the biblical story of the capture of Jericho, the priests were told to walk round the outside of the besieged city carrying trumpets made of rams' horns. Seven priests with seven trumpets had to walk round the walls seven times, and on the seventh day when they blew the trumpets and all the people shouted, the walls came tumbling down. This was surely a tribute not only to the power of the trumpets, but also to the magical properties of the number seven.

Over the centuries, the four families of the orchestra – the strings, the woodwind, the brass, and the percussion – gradually developed from such simple beginnings, and the religious and military associations of music were eventually overtaken by the modern idea of music as a form of pleasure and self-expression.

But although we have outgrown many of the instruments used before about 1600, the twentieth century hasn't turned its back on them. At the beginning of this century, a Frenchman called Arnold Dolmetsch, who had settled in England, became fascinated by old instruments such as the lute and the recorder and taught himself to play them. He revived music that hadn't been played for centuries, and his concerts aroused such interest that he was able to start a workshop where he made copies of the old instruments for the many people who wanted to follow his example and learn to play them. If you have a recorder, the chances are that it will have been made by the firm of Dolmetsch, who are still very active.

More recently, David Munrow, a young music lecturer, became just as fascinated as Dolmetsch by even earlier instruments. He began to collect them, and formed a group called the Early Music Consort of London, which was able to play such unfamiliar instruments as the sackbut, the crumhorn, the rebec, the cornett, the shawm, the chalumeau, and the cittern. Sadly David Munrow died in 1976, when he was still very young, but he left behind a splendid legacy of records. So if you want to hear some

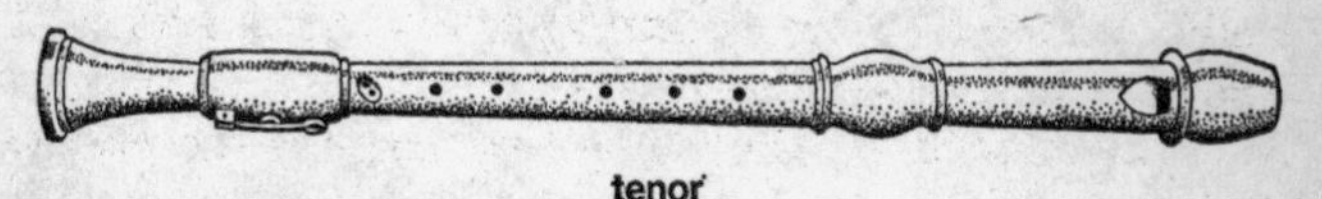

Three recorders

of these intriguing instruments, see if you have any of David Munrow's records at school.

Composers of today have become more adventurous in their use of instruments and sometimes ask players to treat them in an unusual way. String players may have to use the wooden part of the bow instead of the hair, and in one of his string quartets the Russian composer Shostakovich asks a player to tap on his instrument. Not surprisingly, in view of the value of a good instrument, when I heard this performed, the player had brought along an extra violin to tap.

Piano music has become more percussive, and you may now see a pianist disappearing behind the lid of his grand piano in order to strike the keys with a drumstick or pluck them with his fingernails.

Wind players too may have to do something unexpected, such as take out the reed or mouthpiece of their instrument and then either blow through them on their own or play the instrument without them.

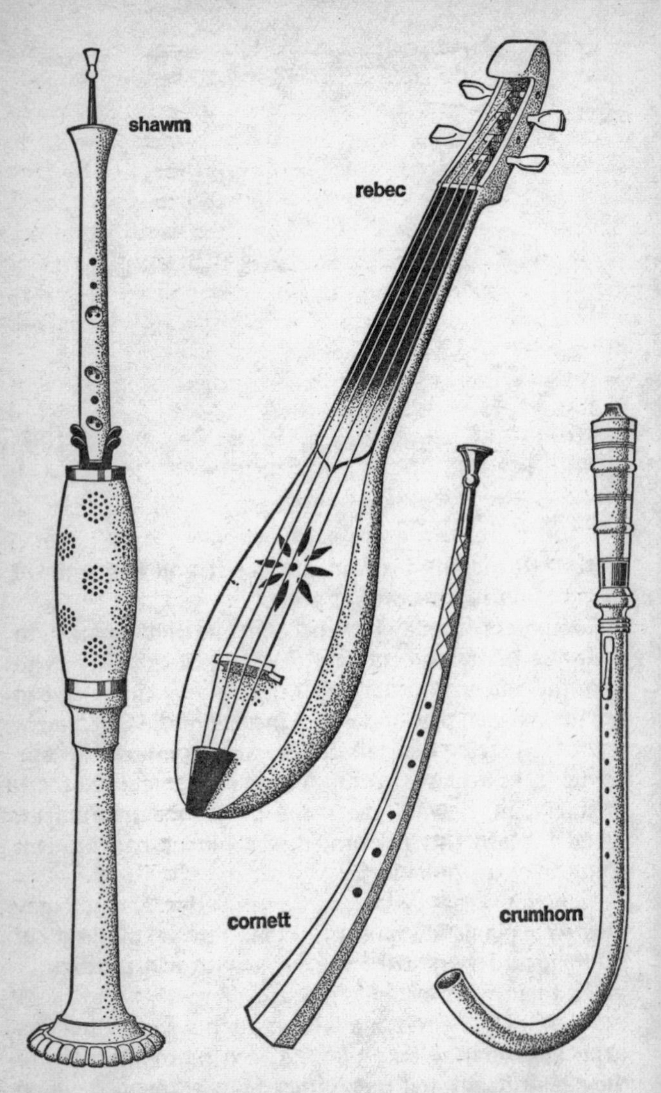

Some medieval musical instruments

Percussion has provided an obvious source for exciting new sounds, and some of them come from extremely ancient instruments such as African drums and Chinese wood blocks. In *Zyklus*, the German composer Stockhausen expects the sole performer to use thirteen different percussion instruments – and he doesn't make his life any easier by leaving him free to start the work wherever he likes and sometimes giving him a choice of notes. This idea of leaving the order of the music to chance is one of the experiments carried out by modern composers such as Stockhausen and John Cage.

Perhaps the most extraordinary 'new sound' is that provided by the American John Cage in a piece called simply *4′ 33″*. It is performed by several musicians and a solo pianist who come on stage and then sit in silence for four minutes thirty-three seconds. It sounds like a joke, but John Cage is a serious composer who sees his 'Silent Sonata' as a chance for the audience to listen consciously to silence and think about it as a work of art.

The invention of the tape-recorder has made it possible to cut sound up, stretch it out and even play it backwards, and in the 1950s a new kind of music – called *musique concrete* in France – began to be created by electronic equipment. The BBC has a Radiophonic Workshop where they can produce an infinite range of sounds with a very sophisticated piece of space-age equipment called a synthesiser, and there they created the best-known piece of electronic music in Britain: the *Dr Who* theme.

But the music I shall be talking about in this book doesn't belong to the space-age, though in its time much of it was considered revolutionary and outrageous. People always find new music difficult to understand because they come to it with very definite ideas about how music should sound, ideas that have been formed by the music they know well. As you won't, as yet, have set ideas about what music should and shouldn't do, you are in the best position to listen to new music, and you'll find that many of the concerts specially organised for you (see Chapter 11) will give you the chance to hear works by composers such as Thea Musgrave, Malcolm Williamson, Peter Maxwell Davies, Richard Rodney Bennett and Gordon Crosse, who are writing today.

For some people, music often conjures up pictures that seem to illustrate it, but unless the composer has made it clear that he is writing descriptive music or telling a story, it is misleading to look for this kind of definite meaning.

The question of what music means and why it gives us pleasure would certainly not have bothered the early composers and musicians. Their music had a very definite purpose: it was used in church to glorify God by ornamenting the daily services and important festivals such as Christmas and Easter, and it was used for dancing and entertaining at feasts and popular celebrations such as weddings. As we shall see, these uses became much more sophisticated and elaborate until some of them came to an end, but music itself went on to get ideas and become capable of expressing all sorts of feelings. Of course the early composers expressed happiness and sadness in their music, but their feelings were not as inward-looking as they became when music shared in the passionate feelings of the Romantic movement and instead of being written mainly for social occasions came more and more to express private solitary moments.

You may not have been aware of music as reflecting the ideas and taste of the time at which it was written, but you have probably noticed how some music seems to suit certain periods. Television often uses music to create the right mood for programmes about art treasures or historic places or plays set in the past, and although you may not have recognised the music as belonging to the same period, you would have noticed if it had not fitted in and contradicted the picture on your screen. There is a link between the theatrical splendour of the churches designed by Nicholas Hawksmoor and the palaces and great houses designed by Sir John Vanbrugh, and the concertos of Bach, Handel and other Baroque composers. In the one you can see ornaments and flourishes in stone, in the other hear these same delights translated into sound.

If you try matching up buildings, paintings, plays, novels, and music with each other, you will soon see that the taste of an age shows itself in all the arts. And this is just as true of today. Many people don't like modern music because they find it harsh and discordant; it doesn't convey the sense of calm and order that they admire in the work of Handel or Mozart. But we are not living in the kind of ordered world that they knew, and so our music expresses the excitement and anxieties of an age in which it isn't safe to take anything for granted and ideas are changing at a rate unknown to a composer such as Haydn. This doesn't mean that all the composers of the past had safe happy lives. Far from it, but although many of them were harassed by unhappiness, disappointment, poverty, and illness, they were able to draw inspiration from certainties that we don't have any more. So much of their music is confident and cheerful, while ours is not.

When music chooses to be descriptive, it is particularly good at portraying the natural world. You can find all sorts of animals, for example, from the lambs, fishes, bees and birds that dart about in Haydn's musical paintings of *The Seasons* to the menagerie in Saint-Saëns' *Carnival of Animals* (which includes lions, cocks and hens, asses, a tortoise, and kangaroos), the baby elephant in Poulenc's *Barber le Petit Elephant*, and the bird, duck, cat, and wolf of Prokofiev's *Peter and the Wolf*. Musical landscapes include the lively Edwardian London of Elgar's *Cockaigne Overture*, the grandeur of Fingal's Cave as seen in Mendelssohn's *Overture to the Hebrides*, and the sparkling *Blue Danube* of Johann Strauss's irresistible waltz.

When you add movement to music, as in ballet, or words, as in songs and opera, music reveals a wonderful ability to evoke places and emotions and to conjure up fantastic worlds. Listen to the way in which Tchaikovsky creates the mysterious magic of his *Swan Lake*. It would take many words by a great writer to achieve the same result.

One of the most unusual subjects described in music was the friends of the composer Edward Elgar. He was doodling on the piano one evening when he made up a tune that his wife rather liked. When he played it again, a little differently, she said that it reminded her of the way one of their friends used to bang the door as he went out of the room. Elgar developed this idea, and his *Enigma Variations* (as he called the work) is a series of musical portraits of his friends, including a young woman with a slight stammer and an organist who had a bulldog that was always falling into the river and then scrambling out with a joyful bark, as you can hear.

But although the *Enigma Variations* has a definite programme, and much has been written about Elgar's friends and about the puzzle he hints at in the title (an enigma is a kind of riddle), you can enjoy the music without knowing anything about the 'friends pictured within'. It stands triumphantly and satisfyingly on its own feet because although Elgar borrowed words from painting to describe what he was doing, when he came to compose the music he moved into a realm of sounds that have a meaning and unity of their own.

Some people have argued that because music has to follow its own rules and these can't be translated into words, it is wrong to talk about the 'meaning' of a sonata or a symphony. They say that we are either giving our own interpretation to the music, or accepting someone else's, instead of realising that music forms sound patterns of balance and contrast that are pleasing in themselves but don't have any special significance.

This is certainly true of some music, but the greatest music does also seem to express deep feelings, and composers themselves don't seem to think of their music as something that is quite apart from the rest of their lives. Where letters, diaries, and notebooks have survived, they often give direct proof of the way in which composers have felt that they were expressing their feelings and experiences in their music.

When he was about seven or eight, Elgar was once found sitting on the river bank with a pencil and some music paper. Asked what he was up to, he said that he was 'trying to write down what the reeds were saying'. He later explained the mysterious process of writing music – mysterious, that is, to most of us, who don't have tunes in our heads – by saying that he had musical daydreams just as other people had dreams about heroes and adventures, and that he could express almost any thought in terms of music.

Another far less traditional composer, Anton von Webern, who was one of the first people to experiment with atonal music, said that an experience went round and round inside him until it came out as music. People who still feel that his music is too experimental might be surprised to know that he thought of it as reflecting such events as his mother's death, and spoke of being inspired by the scenery and flowers of the mountains and the sight of children playing in the snow.

So look out in music not only for pleasing tunes and the patterns made by building themes and variations on them into contrasting movements, but also for reflections of the time at which the composer lived, the range of instruments he had at his disposal, and his personal experiences. The more you know about such things and about the way in which music was made and is made today, the more opportunities you will have for looking at music from different points of view, most of them not technical, and for discovering in it ideas and feelings that are an important – some people would say the most important – part of the way we live.

2 *Signs for sounds*

Before looking at the various families of instruments that make up the orchestra and seeing how they work together, we need to get a few technicalities out of the way. These will be kept to a minimum, but a little knowledge of the special language used for the sounds of music will stop you from feeling that the technical side is a complete mystery.

Music is made up of sounds, sounds that may make our pulse beat faster or cause our hair to stand on end. But what exactly is sound and what produces it? Sound starts with some form of motion or vibration that causes sound waves to travel through the air from the vibrating object to our ear. We then hear these vibrations as sound.

What kind of sound it is will depend on what the object is made of and how fast it is vibrating. The number of vibrations per second are described by the word frequency, and if a sound has a high frequency (lots of vibrations per second), it will produce a high note, and if it has a low frequency, a low note. Human beings can't hear a note that is lower than about twenty vibrations per second or higher than about 20,000 vibrations per second, but a dog will be able to hear a whistle that is too high for us.

Many vibrations make a sound that can only be called a noise, but if the frequency of the vibration is regular, it will make a sound that we can recognise as a definite note. The notes of music each have their own frequency, and in order for musicians to be able to play together without some of them sounding out of tune, they have to make sure that the same notes have the same frequency. At an international conference in 1939, most of the Western nations agreed that the note a′ should have 440 vibrations per second, and if you listen carefully at the beginning of a concert, you will hear all the players tuning their instruments to this A, which is usually played by the oboe. (The diagram on page 28 shows you where to find a′ on the keyboard. You will see that there is a special way – C, c, °c′, and so on – of indicating the notes in each octave.)

Although notes are identified by their characteristic frequency, when we call them A or C, for example, we are only referring to their lowest sound or *fundamental*. When making this sound, each instrument will also at the same time produce a number of fainter, higher sounds which are called *overtones*.

The interesting thing about overtones is that they vary from one instrument to another, and they are responsible for giving each instrument its distinctive sound. The flute, for instance, has very faint overtones and so sounds very pure, but the oboe has plenty of high overtones that colour its sound and make it different from that of the saxophone, which has more low overtones. This may sound complicated, but I'm sure you won't mistake a violin for a trumpet, and it is hearing the difference between the various instruments that really counts. Knowing why is for those of you who like scientific explanations.

Music goes back far beyond the time when people were able to write it down, and folk-songs are a good example of the kind of music that was passed on, by ear, from one generation to the next. But most of the music we shall be concerned with belongs to a fairly recent period of history, from the sixteenth century onwards, and it has been handed down to us in written form.

In order to write down a piece of music, signs were needed to indicate the pitch of a note (that is, how high or low it is), the volume of a note (how loud or soft it is), and the length of a note (how long it lasts). The system of lines and spaces used today was invented by a Benedictine monk, Guido d'Arezzo, who lived at the end of the tenth century. He suggested using three or four lines to show the rise and fall of notes, and later on this became the five-line staff used now.

The notes are placed on the lines and spaces of the staff, and one staff is used for the notes above middle C (so-called because it comes roughly in the middle of the piano keyboard) and another for the notes below middle C. The top staff is called the *treble clef*, and it is marked with a sign that was originally a capital G because it circles round the second line, the line that represents the note G. The bottom staff, the *bass clef*, is marked by a sign that was originally a capital F, and the line for F is shown by two dots on either side of it. (There are other clefs too, but the treble and bass are the most common.)

The treble and bass clefs with middle C marked in between them

Another sign you will see on the staff, usually at the beginning of a piece, are two figures one above the other like a fraction. This is the time signature, and the top figure shows how many beats there are in a bar (music is divided up into equal units called bars) while the bottom figure shows how long each beat should last.

A composer will also want to indicate the speed of the music, and he does this either by using words such as *grave* (which means very slow) and *prestissimo* (as fast as possible) or by giving a metronome mark. The metronome, which was invented at the beginning of the nineteenth century, is an instrument that measures the number of beats per minute at any given speed. So if a composer were to mark his score ♩ = 60 it would mean that he wanted sixty crotchet beats a minute.

To show how loud or soft the music should be, a composer will use abbreviations such as ppp, mp, mf, ff, which stand for *molto pianissimo* (extremely soft), *mezzo piano* (fairly soft), *mezzo forte* (fairly loud) and *fortissimo* (very loud). And if you're wondering why musical terms are always in Italian, it's because for a long time Italy was the leading country for music.

Notes are represented by little black and white oval signs with stems and tails, and they tell us the pitch of a sound and how long it should last. The longest note is the semibreve, and this can be divided into two minims, or four crotchets, or eight quavers, or sixteen semiquavers, or thirty-two demisemiquavers. They look like this:

Pitch is indicated by the first seven letters of the alphabet, but instead of the first note being A, for some reason it is C. So the musical alphabet goes C D E F G A B and then starts at C again. The interval (or distance) between each note and its namesake above or below is called an *octave*, because it has eight (Latin: *octo*) steps if you count both the top and bottom notes. You can hear the special relationship between two notes an octave apart if you play them together. They will sound different and yet somehow the same, and this is because the top note has twice as many vibrations as the note an octave below. We hear this mathematical relationship by instinct, but it can also be expressed in figures, so that if middle C, for example, has a frequency of 256, the frequency of the C above it will be 512 and of the C below it 128.

A series of eight notes known as a *scale* (from the Latin *scala*, which means a ladder) can be built on each note in the musical alphabet, and it is easiest to see how these scales are arranged by looking at the keyboard of a piano.

As you can see on page 28, the keyboard can be divided into octaves, and the lowest octave has been marked with the letters of the musical alphabet. Notice that the black and white notes form a special pattern: there is a black note between C and D and D and E, but not between E and F or B and C. This black note represents a halfway stage between those white notes that are a whole tone apart. In Western music the smallest distance between two tones is a semitone, and each note on the keyboard is a semitone above or below the note next to it when you include the black notes too. So from C to the black note above it is a semitone, from the black note to D is a semitone, and from E to F is also a semitone.

Scales can be built upwards or downwards from any note, and it is the position of the tones and semitones that decides what kind of scale it is.

The keyboard is divided into octaves. The notation shows their positions when written down

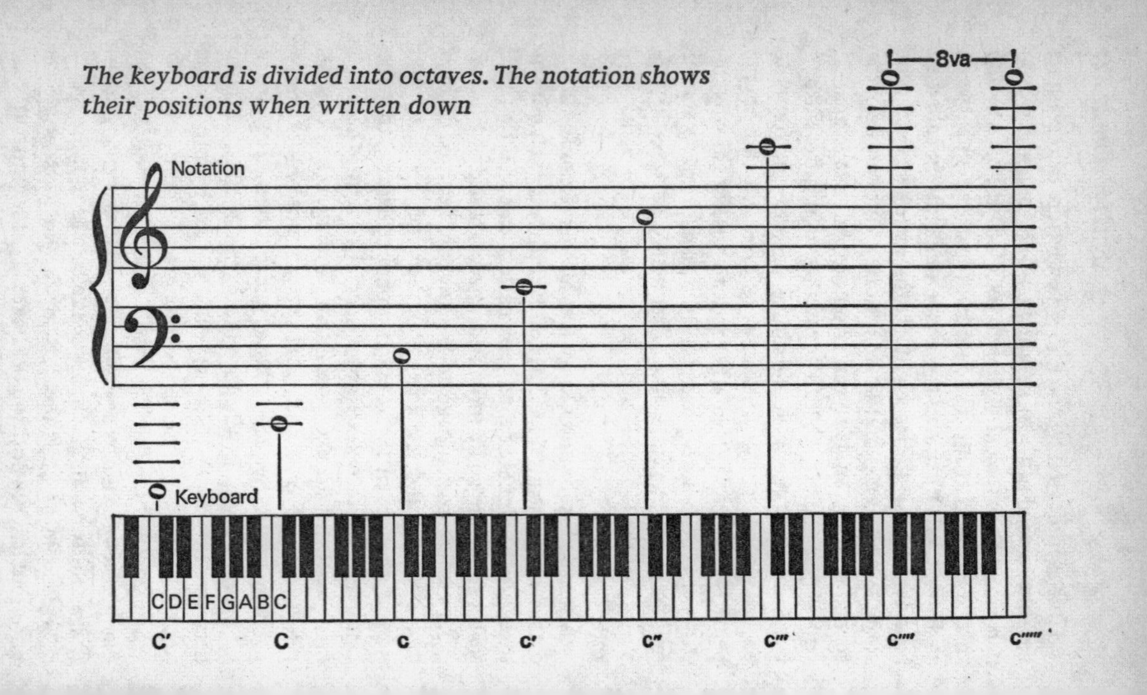

Suppose, for example, we decide to build our scale on C and go up the keyboard on the notes marked in the diagram. We are using only the white keys, and the distances between them give us two groups of four notes, each of which has a semitone between the third and fourth notes, so that it looks like this:

Scale of C major

This is the characteristic pattern of a *major scale.*

You can build a major scale on any note, but you'll have to make certain changes so that it is still the same shape. Supposing you decide to start on A. The first two notes A and B are a tone apart, so that's all right, but then comes a problem. B and C are only a semitone apart whereas the pattern calls for a tone, so you're a semitone short. You can make this up by using the black note above C, but as you need a C in your scale you'll have to call this note C sharp. The distance between C sharp and D is a semitone, which is right for the pattern, but there are more problems when you get to E. F has to be raised to F sharp to provide a whole tone, and then G has to become G sharp to complete the pattern. You end up with a scale that has the same shape as C major, but to

Scale of A major

produce this you have had to raise (or sharpen) three notes: C, F and G.

All the major scales except C major need at least one note sharpened (raised by a semitone) or flattened (lowered by a semitone) to preserve the right pattern, and these sharps and flats are indicated by signs like this:

♯ sharp ♭ flat

Music would look rather confusing if all the sharps and flats had to be marked separately, so they are usually grouped together at the beginning of each line. They are called the *key-signature,* and they indicate the set of notes, or *key*, on which the piece is built.

If you're learning music, you probably already know quite a lot about scales and the way they relate to each other, and have come across other scales with a slightly different pattern called *minor scales*. Every note has its own major and minor scales, but the relationship between them isn't as straightforward as you might think. It doesn't depend on the major and minor scales starting on the same note, but on their both having the same key signature, that is, the same number of sharps or flats. So the relative minor of C major is not C minor, which has three flats in it, but A minor, which like C major doesn't have any sharps or flats at all. You can work out the relative minor of any major key by remembering that the last three notes of the major scale become the first three notes of its relative minor.

The first note of any scale is the most important. It is called the *tonic* or *keynote,* and it gives its name to the scale or piece of music built round it. All tonal music is written within the key system and usually centres round a particular key. Thus a piece will be described as being in C major or some other key because the notes of that key play an important part in it.

The key system has given composers a framework for their music. From the second half of the sixteenth century until the beginning of the twentieth century, they used it when writing music much as we use grammar when speaking or writing. We all take this tonal system for granted, even if we're not really aware of it until we miss it in the works of composers such as Schoenberg, Webern and Boulez, who experimented with a different system.

Schoenberg put aside the major-minor key system, in which some notes are more important than others, in favour of treating all the twelve notes of the octave (the seven white and five black notes that we saw on our keyboard octave) as equal. The twelve notes were arranged in a particular order for each work, and although this order could then be played about with and perhaps turned upside down or back to front, some relationship to the original order was preserved all through the work. Many people don't like such *atonal* or keyless music, and even without knowing anything about the technicalities they feel instinctively that it goes against their sense of what sounds right.

One of the places where you will come across references to keys is in the titles of works, such as Beethoven's *Symphony No. 5 in C minor* or Tchaikovsky's *Piano Concerto No. 1 in B flat minor*. The idea of using the key in which the first movement was written to identify the piece as a whole started with the court orchestras of the seventeenth and eighteenth centuries. The players often found themselves faced with concertos and symphonies that lacked distinctive titles, and so they would refer to them among themselves as the one in D major or G major, even though the rest of the work might be in some other key. They were only concerned with finding the right piece in the first place, and although players don't have the same problem today, the old convention is still used.

The choice of key depends on the kind of mood the composer wants to create and on the sort of instruments he plans to use. At one time, some instruments could only be played in certain keys, and D major was very popular in the eighteenth century because it was the home key of trumpets and horns.

As instruments were improved and the choice of keys in which they could be played became wider, composers began to use certain keys because they felt that they were particularly suitable for certain kinds of music. Thus C minor was felt to be dark and dramatic (think of Beethoven's *Fifth Symphony*) and D major rather military and right for grand occasions (Handel's *Music for the Royal Fireworks* and Elgar's 'Land of Hope and Glory' march), while E flat major was serious and sorrowful and suggested beautiful solemn melodies such as those in Beethoven's *Eroica Symphony* and *Emperor Concerto*.

As well as being identified by keys, composers' works are also often referred to by an opus number. *Opus* is the Latin word for *work*, and it is used in this sense to indicate the order in which the works were published. So a composer's first published work would be his opus (usually shortened to Op.) 1, and so on. The opus number should give you a rough idea of the order in which the works were written, but early works were often not published at the time and then brought out years later, so op. numbers can be very unreliable.

To correct this, when music began to be studied seriously, scholars tried to sort some composers' works into proper order and re-number them. A famous example of this was the great catalogue of Mozart's music produced by Ludwig Ritte von Köchel. It was published in 1862, and since then Mozart's works have always been identified by their K. number. His little Serenade in G for strings is K.525 – you probably know it better as *Eine Kleine Nachtmusik*.

Many scholars since have followed Köchel's example – Schubert's music is now identified by D. numbers, the work of Otto Erich Deutsch – and you will see similar letters and numbers being used in concert programmes in place of the old op. numbers.

But keys and op. numbers aren't easy to remember, so no wonder many famous pieces of music have acquired popular nicknames. The *Moonlight Sonata* or the *New World Symphony* are certainly more memorable titles than *Sonata in C sharp minor Op. 27/2* or *Symphony No. 9 in E minor, Op. 95*.

Some nicknames come from the name of the composer's patron – Bach's *Brandenburg Concertos* were written for the Margrave of Brandenburg – or from the place that inspired the music or where it was written, such as Mendelssohn's *Scottish* and *Italian* symphonies, but some don't have much connection with the music. Scarlatti's *Sonata in G minor*, for example, is known as the *Cat's Fugue* because the composer is said to have been inspired by a cat walking across the keyboard of his harpsichord.

Not surprisingly, perhaps, in view of all the music he wrote including a hundred and four symphonies, the composer whose works have the most nicknames is Haydn. Some of them were supplied by him, others by various publishers, and the names given to his symphonies include *The Farewell, The Philosopher, The Schoolmaster, The Bear, The Hen, The Oxford, The Surprise, The Miracle, The Clock* and *The London*.

It's easy to guess the origin of some of these names, but if you're stuck, or would like to find out more about musical nicknames in general, there is a full list of them complete with explanations where they're known in *The Guinness Book of Music Facts & Feats*.

3 Stringed instruments

The history of musical instruments cannot be told only in terms of music, because as you will soon see, the way in which they developed depended not only on their musical capabilities but also on the composers who wrote (or didn't write) for them, on the taste of the people who played them and listened to them, and on the talent of individual players, some of whom were so gifted that they extended the range of their instrument and thus inspired composers to write more difficult works for them. There were also the instrument-makers whose skill and devotion produced instruments so beautiful that they inspired composers and performers, and thus the cycle of new developments and greater possibilities rolled on.

The strings were not the first instruments to be invented – though angels are often shown playing harps – but you will recognise them at once if you've been to a concert. They sit at the front of the stage, nearest to the conductor, and there are so many of them and the sound they make is so important in all orchestral music that they have a good claim to be considered first.

The violin family – and here we are talking about all four members, the violin, the viola, the cello, and the double-bass – are the most beautiful pieces of musical furniture. They are made of wood – and the particular kind of wood, its thickness, and the way it has been varnished, is very important – and all four have a characteristic rounded shape with a curving nipped-in waist, a long thin neck ending in a carved scroll, two long narrow sound-holes in the shape of a letter f, and set between them a bridge over which the strings are stretched.

There are four strings, and they are attached to the tailpiece at the bottom and at the top to pegs which can be turned to sharpen or flatten the pitch of a string. The sound is produced by vibrating the strings, and in the violin family this is done either with the fingers or with a bow, a slightly curving stick with horsehair stretched across it. Each string sounds one note, and the other notes are made by pressing the string against the fingerboard so that only a part of it is free to vibrate. The pitch varies according to the length of the string, and the rule is the shorter the string, the higher the note. So if the player wants a low note, he or she will press the string down right at the top of the fingerboard.

Plucking the strings with the fingers produces a different effect known as pizzicato, and the volume and tone quality can be varied by using the wood or the bow instead of the hair, by bowing near the bridge or above the fingerboard, and by trilling on the same note. The tone can also be muted, or softened, by attaching a special little gadget called a mute to the bridge.

The violin

No one is quite sure which instrument was the direct ancestor of the violin. We know from early paintings of angels and minstrels that there were various stringed instruments such as the rebec and the Renaissance fiddle, but they were not the same as the violin, and yet when it first appeared in northern Italy around the middle of the

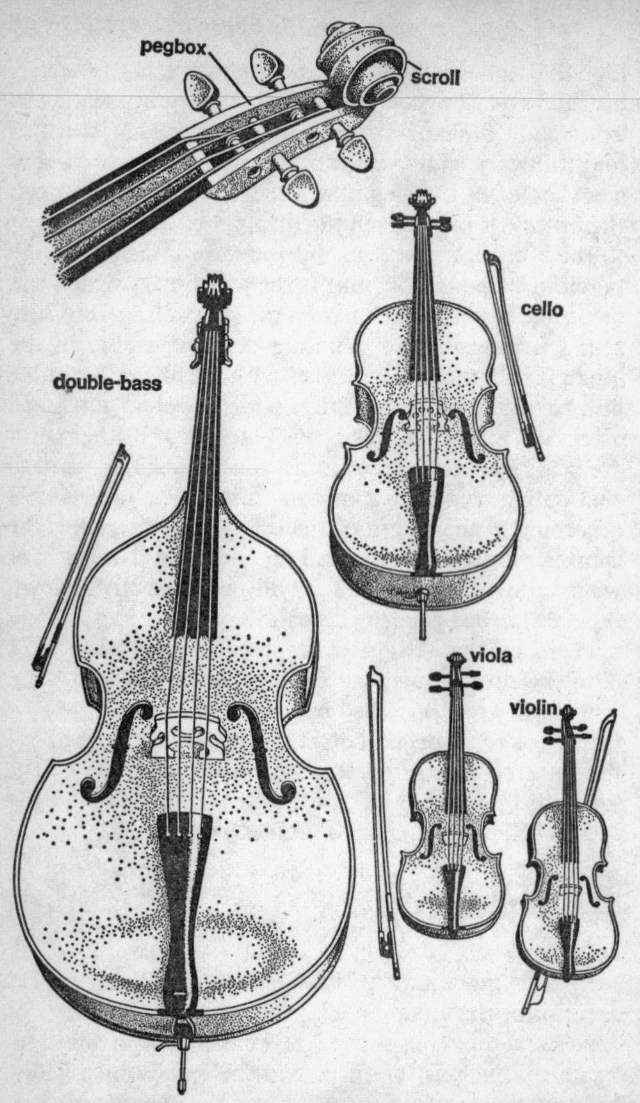

The violin family with (top) the neck of the violin showing the pegbox and scroll

sixteenth century, the violin was recognisably the same instrument it is today. If you look at any early violins in a museum, you'll see that their shape hasn't changed much over the years, though the way they are played has. The early violins were propped up against the player's chest instead of held over the shoulder, as they are today.

We live in a world where the latest, most up-to-date model is often considered the best, but this is not the case with the violin. Just as certain wine is improved by keeping, so musicians have found that the most beautiful sounds come from violins that were made several centuries ago.

The earliest violins that survive today were all made in the little town of Cremona in northern Italy, where the instrument-making tradition seems to have started with the Amati family some time during the sixteenth century. Andrea Amati made a violin that was later used by the virtuoso player and composer Arcangelo Corelli, who helped to make the violin popular by his fiery performances and by writing a number of sonatas and concertos for it.

Andrea passed his skill on to his sons and his grandsons. Nicolo Amati not only made fine instruments himself but had a number of famous pupils including the great Stradivari, acknowledged to be the greatest maker of violins and cellos who ever lived. Sadly we don't know much about him, except that he worked in Cremona, lived to be over ninety, and made hundreds of superb instruments, some of which are still being played. Today a Stradivarius is worth thousands of pounds – a violin auctioned in 1979 fetched £145,000.

Such a high price reflects not only the scarcity value of the instruments – there are thought to be about sixty Stradivarius cellos still in existence – but above all the unique, beautiful quality of their sound. Of course experts have examined them very carefully. They have studied the design, the exact placing of the various parts, the amount of air inside, the wood, the varnish, but they have not been able to discover Stradivari's secret. Time may have had something to do with it, because his instruments are known to have needed time to mature and some of the large ones took up to eighty years to produce their best tone; it may have been the wood he chose or the climate of the area where he lived, but it was probably above all the fact that his skill as a craftsman has never been equalled.

For nearly two hundred years all the best violins came from Cremona and their fame was spread by virtuoso players. The craft gradually moved to other centres, to Mantua and Venice, to Florence, Bologna, Rome, Naples, Milan, and eventually to places outside Italy, to Germany, France and England, but the Italian makers of the seventeenth and eighteenth centuries remained supreme and their products always commanded the highest prices. It became the fashion for other makers to copy them and to label their instruments with their names, not in order to deceive but as a compliment to designs that were acknowledged to be the best.

The greatest maker of bows, however, was not an Italian but a Frenchman, François Tourte. The early players had used straight bows, but Tourte perfected a way of bending the wood by heating it and established the curving shape still used. Interestingly, although it is easy to overlook the bow, some players rate a fine bow as even more important than a fine instrument.

The violin is the smallest member of the violin family and the one with the highest voice. Its strings are tuned g, d′, a′, e″, and it has a range of more than three and a half octaves, which means that it can sound any note from the G below middle C right up to almost the furthest end of the keyboard (see page 28).

It started life as a rather lowly instrument that was despised by the well-to-do amateur player, who thought the viol (which was a similar shape, had six strings, and was held on or between the knees) was a much more refined instrument.

So the violin, or fiddle as it was popularly called, was left to servants such as the dancing-master and wandering fiddler, and they taught it jigs, pavans, galliards and all kinds of other dances. The violin made itself heard. It began to replace the rebec at weddings and festivals, it was used for dances at court, and eventually it even made its way into church.

Its progress was helped by a new style of writing music that was more suited to the violin than the viol and that enabled instruments to take over from the voice, which until then had been supreme in music. Music also began to free itself from the dictates of the church and to develop forms that were meant for entertainment rather than worship. There were suites and sonatas that strung together many of the old dances, there was the beginning of opera and ballet, and there were numerous concertos for string orchestra, especially by Vivaldi, who holds the record for having written more concertos (nearly five hundred) than anyone else.

Why did he write so many? It was all part of his job as the director of music at an orphanage for girls in Venice. At one stage he had a contract to write two concertos a month, and many of them were probably written in a great hurry and not meant to be played more than once. Some were obviously written to suit the capabilities of his students, but Vivaldi was a great violinist himself and he realised how effective it was to single out one player and give him a dazzling, impressive part. So he not only wrote concertos that showed the different effects that could be achieved by a small string orchestra but also developed the solo concerto.

His example was followed by an even greater composer, J. S. Bach, who wrote one of the most beautiful double violin concertos of this period. The two violins repeat and echo each other, weaving together simple tunes that are deeply moving. Bach also wrote six very fine sonatas for violin and harpsichord.

The grave seriousness of Bach and his contemporary Handel gave way to a taste for light-hearted, graceful melody. It became fashionable for bands of musicians to play under the windows of gentlemen and their friends, and *serenades, divertimenti, nocturnes* or night-music – heard at their best in the work of Mozart – were typical of this kind of gay outdoor music.

The violin played a leading part in this, and also in the string quartet – small-scale music ideal for the drawing room – which was developed by Haydn and perfected by Mozart. They also developed the symphony (see page 110), and the violin and the other strings were to provide the backbone of the symphony orchestra.

As we shall see with other instruments, their popularity always increases when a really outstanding player appears. The genius of the violin was to be an extraordinary player called Niccolò Paganini, who was thought to be inspired by the devil. He had a wonderful violin made by one of the greatest old Italian masters, Guarneri del Gesu, and he travelled round Europe giving concerts that attracted huge audiences. His playing and his personality were sensational, and he looked the part of the inspired musician with his long hair, piercing eyes, and strange haunted expression. He usually played music that he had written himself, music that gave him the star part and displayed his amazing technique. It is seldom heard nowadays, but a piece he wrote at the age of nineteen was to inspire Rachmaninov's *Rhapsody on a Theme of Paganini*.

The violin had become a more powerful instrument

The brilliant violinist Paganini

and the whole orchestra was growing in volume and tone-colour, a development encouraged by Beethoven in his concertos and symphonies. Soloists had to work hard to stay in the picture, and the great violin concertos of the nineteenth century, by Beethoven, Mendelssohn, Brahms, and Tchaikovsky, call for brilliant playing.

The only twentieth-century violin concerto to rival them is Elgar's *Concerto in B minor*, dedicated to the famous Austrian violinist Fritz Kreisler, who gave the first performance of it in 1910. In 1932, when the Gramophone Company wanted to record it with the composer conducting, they chose Yehudi Menuhin, then only sixteen, as the soloist – and the recording is still available. Elgar's concerto has also inspired wonderful performances by Pinchas Zukerman and the young Korean player Kyung-Wha Chung, who is one of the most exciting violinists of today.

Other players to look out for are David Oistrakh, who died in 1974 but made many fine recordings, Itzhak Perlman, and Josef Suk, the great-grandson of the composer Dvorak. The violin may not seem a natural for jazz, but if you want to hear what it can do, listen to the records of Joe Venuti or Stephane Grappelly.

If you're learning the violin, spare a thought for the pupils of the Japanese teacher Dr Suzuki. He claims that anyone can play the violin, providing they start early enough – and his pupils start at the age of three. They learn at first by copying their mother, who has to take lessons too, and achieve remarkable results. But in the early stages they often spend up to a year on one piece. Would you be so patient?

The viola

For a long time the viola was far outshone by its little sister the violin. This seems unfair because they look alike, though the viola is a little bigger and its voice a little deeper, and they were made by the same instrument-makers including Stradivari, though fewer violas were made because there was much less demand for them.

This wasn't surprising because the viola was kept very much in the background. It wasn't needed in trio-sonatas – one of the most popular forms of composition in the early eighteenth century – and it wasn't an instrument that appealed to any of the well-to-do amateurs who liked to patronise music. The truth is that the viola-player was a figure of fun and was often spoken of as someone who wasn't skilful enough to play the violin.

But this attitude gradually changed because two of the eighteenth-century's greatest composers, Haydn and Mozart, both played the viola and so were aware of its rich tone. Haydn gave it important and interesting parts in his string quartets, and Mozart promoted the viola to equal soloist with the violin in his lovely *Sinfonia Concertante*.

Then in the nineteenth century the French composer Berlioz gave the viola its first big Romantic part in his symphony *Harold in Italy*. The work was originally written for Paganini, who had asked Berlioz for a piece in which he could show off his Stradivarius viola. Berlioz did his best and thought he had found a new way of contrasting the viola with the orchestra, but Paganini was disappointed that he wasn't to be the centre of attention all the time and so he declined to play.

But the viola still wasn't officially a solo instrument, and it had to wait until an outstanding player turned up. There was no one teaching or learning the viola when Lionel Tertis went to the Royal Academy of Music in 1896, but he soon changed this. He made himself such a fine player that he became principal viola in Henry Wood's orchestra overnight, and his brilliant playing soon attracted pupils and inspired Vaughan Williams and Gustav Holst to write works for him.

Other composers to write specially for the viola include William Walton and Béla Bartók, who wrote a concerto for the fine player William Primrose, a Scotsman who went to live in the United States.

The viola's strings are tuned c g d′ a′, and its range is just over three octaves.

The cello

This is big brother. It's the same shape as the violin and the viola, but too big for the player to hold on his shoulder so it rests between his knees and balances on a metal spike known as an end pin. This spike wasn't used until late in the nineteenth century and this is why all the early cellists were men. Apart from the sheer weight of the instrument, it was thought unladylike to straddle a cello – ladies always rode horses side-saddle not astride – and although one or two ladies tried to play side-saddle it wasn't a great success.

The cello's full name is violoncello, but it is always called by the short form nowadays. Its strings are tuned C G d a (like the viola but an octave lower), and it can go as low as two octaves below middle C and as high as nearly two octaves above. Its voice is rich and warm and has been described as like brown velvet.

The cello came on the scene a little later than the violin and the viola. At first, like them, it was a humble instrument used in processions and for dancing, but before long it began to take the place of the more fashionable bass gamba.

It really came into its own as a continuo instrument playing a bass accompaniment. During the seventeenth century it was the fashion for composers to write down only the bass-line of an accompaniment and leave the player to work out the rest of the harmony. Sometimes he was helped by figures indicating the other parts needed, and this was known as a figured bass. The upper parts were played by a lute or a keyboard instrument, but the actual bass-notes were often left to the cello or the double-bass. You can hear what this sounded like if you listen to the songs in early operas or to much of the instrumental music of this period.

As with the violin, composers began to write sonatas and concertos for the cello, and the first composer to write a solo concerto was the industrious Vivaldi. He wrote twenty-seven cello concertos, but some of them weren't much more than exercises for his students.

As the cello became more important, outstanding players increased its popularity, and during the eighteenth century its fame spread from Italy to the rest of Europe and on to the United States.

As the style of music changed, so did the role of the cello. It was used to accompany singers, in the orchestra, and above all in the string quartets of Haydn, Mozart, and Beethoven, which were to give the cellist his greatest opportunities.

The Italian player Luigi Boccherini (best-known today for his charming minuet) wrote four cello concertos, only one of which is still played, and Haydn probably wrote more than the four by him which have survived and include the famous *Concerto in D major*.

More than two hundred cello concertos were written in the nineteenth century, but few of them are still worth playing. The only ones you are likely to hear are those by Schumann and Saint-Saëns, and the beautiful concerto by Dvorak. In the second movement the cello sings a song that was a favourite of Dvorak's sister-in-law. He had been in love with her when they were young, and she died while he was writing the concerto. It is the greatest cello concerto, and once you've heard it you won't need any further convincing of the instrument's nobility and eloquence.

Other cello music to look out for includes five sonatas by Beethoven (especially *No. 3 in A major*), two by Brahms, and the haunting concerto by Elgar, written towards the end of his life when he was feeling sad at the decline of his powers and unhappy that the First World War had destroyed civilisation as he knew it.

The greatest cellist of modern times was Pablo Casals, who revolutionised the whole approach to the instrument. His teaching methods were adopted by players all over the world, and he used his music to try and further the cause of peace. Casals lived to a great age and went on playing the cello into his nineties.

The outstanding performer of today is the Russian

Mstislav Rostropovitch, whose superb playing has inspired a number of composers including Prokofiev and Britten. The most promising British cellist, Jacqueline Du Pré, had to stop playing when she was struck down by illness, but you can get a good idea of her passionate style from her many records. Other fine players include Pierre Fournier, Leonard Rose, and Paul Tortelier.

The double bass

This is the largest member of the violin family and it's so tall that the player has to sit on a high stool to reach it.

Its strings are tuned G D A E, and it can play nearly three octaves with a gruff voice that goes down almost to the bottom of the keyboard. But this has not been low enough for some composers, and you may see basses with an extra string so that they can play the B below bottom E.

Unlike the rest of the violin family, the bass is a descendant of the viols, and their influence can still be seen in its sloping shoulders and flat back. The oldest surviving instrument was made by Gasparo da Salo of Brescia, a fine Italian instrument-maker whose skill helped the bass to better the violone, the largest of the viols, and take its place in the orchestra.

The double-bass's size inspired some makers to produce real monsters. One was so large that it took two men to play it – one of them stopped the strings while the other bowed – and one was so tall that its head went right through the ceiling (via a specially-cut hole) and it had to be tuned from the room above. The Victoria and Albert Museum in London has a giant double-bass more than seven feet tall that once belonged to the great Italian player Domenico Dragonetti, the only man ever to become really famous as a double-bass player. He was a friend of Beethoven, and he came to live in London and actually wrote some solos for the bass.

But even his playing didn't inspire any double-bass concertos, and the instrument has been content to stay in the background, grumbling away below the cellos and providing valuable harmonic support. It also plays in dance bands and jazz groups (Charlie Mingus was a star bassist), when it is usually plucked rather than bowed.

Although the last two instruments in this chapter aren't part of the orchestra, they often turn up at solo recitals, playing with small groups or, in the case of the guitar, as the soloist with an orchestra.

The lute and guitar

The kind of guitar you may have seen Julian Bream or John Williams playing didn't reach its final shape until late in the nineteenth century, but some form of guitar was played by the Hittites, an ancient people who lived more than three thousand years ago.

One of its direct ancestors was the vihuela, a Spanish instrument shaped rather like a guitar that had six sets of double strings, The vihuela had a very short life and disappeared at the end of the sixteenth century, but some of the music written for it is played today by the guitar.

Another ancestor, the lute, remained popular until the eighteenth century and was much in demand in the great houses of the aristocracy and at court. The skilled lutanist knew how to match his master's moods with lively dances or sad love songs of the kind asked for by the Duke Orsino in Shakespeare's *Twelfth Night*, when he called to his musicians:

If music be the food of love, play on;

The lute has a round bowl-shaped back and is more difficult to play than the guitar, which is probably why it went out of fashion, but it inspired much enchanting and often melancholy music, such as that by the great English lutanist John Dowland.

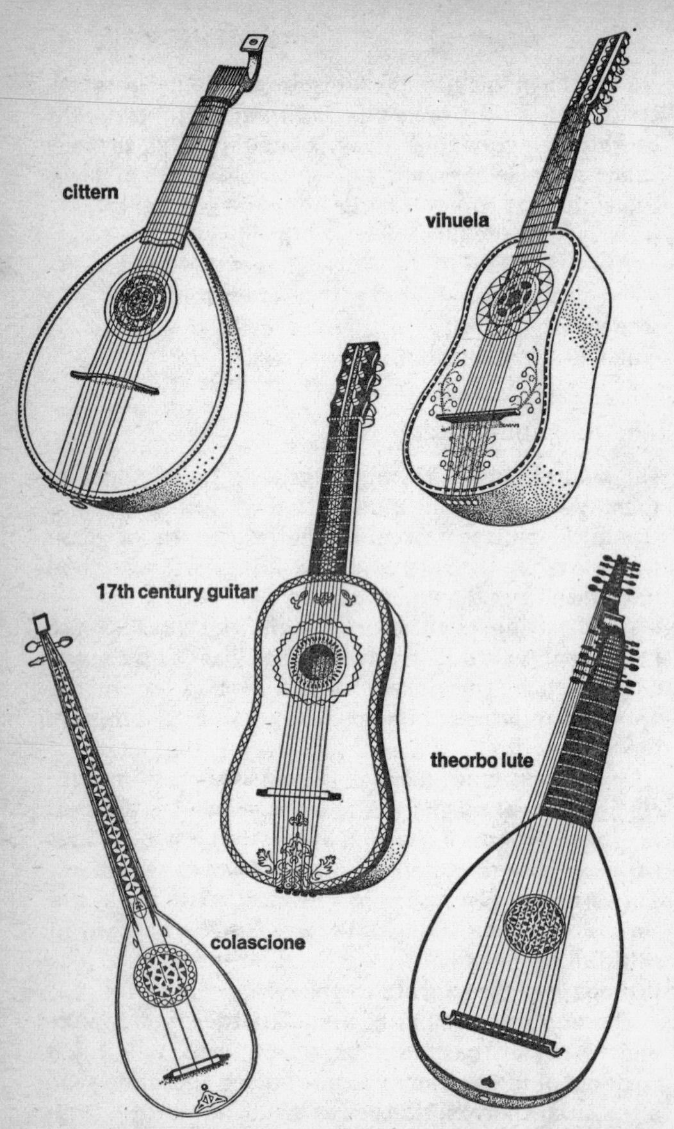

An early guitar with some of its ancestors and relations

But the lute gradually faded away, perhaps because it was so difficult to play; no more music was written for it after about 1780. It wasn't heard again until the end of the nineteenth century, when Arnold Dolmetsch, whom we met on page 14, came across a beautiful old lute made of ebony and ivory at a sale. Dolmetsch couldn't really afford to buy it, but he was so angry when someone made an insulting bid for it that he shouted out, 'Five pounds, you idiot. It's worth fifty' – and the auctioneer promptly knocked it down to him.

Dolmetsch repaired the lute, taught himself to play it, and found a whole new world of 'lost' music, much of which had not been heard for over two hundred years. His playing roused a new interest in the lute, and in recent years the records of players like Julian Bream and Walter Gerwig have brought back to life the airs and dances that charmed and soothed the first Elizabethans and amused the elegant French court.

But if the lute was mainly for professional musicians, the guitar became increasingly popular with amateur players. Various changes took place in its size and shape and the strings finally became the six (tuned E A d g b e) used today.

The beginning of the nineteenth century was a golden age of brilliant players, teachers, and composers, and they transformed the guitar and made it worthy of the concert platform. Among the most important composers were Fernando Sor and Mauro Giuliani, whose pieces are often played today. All sorts of people took up the guitar, from royalty to kitchenmaids (one young woman was turned down for a job because she told her employer that she wanted time off to learn the guitar), but most of them couldn't begin to equal the skill of the great players. They didn't want to play difficult music anyway, but simply to strum an accompaniment to a song, and there was a demand for easy music and teaching books that offered short cuts. Then the piano took over as the ideal instrument for all the family.

But the guitar was to make a triumphant comeback in the twentieth century, thanks to the dazzling example of the great Spanish guitarist Andrés Segovia, whose superb technique inspired composers from all over the world. There was Manuel de Falla from Spain, Manuel Ponce from Mexico, Heitor Villa-Lobos from Brazil, Mario Castelnuovo-Tedesco from Italy, and another Spaniard, Joaquin Rodrigo, whose *Concierto de Aranjuez* is one of the most popular modern concertos.

Following Segovia, guitarists also began to look back to the past for music that could be adapted to the guitar. They found that some of the pieces by Scarlatti, Frescobaldi, Rameau, Couperin and Bach, that had originally been written for the clavichord or the harpsichord, sounded just as pleasing on the guitar.

Two British composers who have written music for the guitar are Malcolm Arnold and Benjamin Britten, whose *Nocturnal* is one of the greatest works for the guitar. As well as Bream and Williams, look out for records by Manuel Barrueco, Narciso Yepes, and the Romeros brothers, Angel and Pepe.

So far we have been talking about the classical guitar, which is shaped like a rather fat figure eight, has a long neck, a fingerboard running down to the soundhole, six strings, and a range of more than three octaves. It is played sitting down, with the guitar resting on the player's thighs, and the strings are stopped by the left hand and plucked by the right.

A different kind of guitar is used for Spanish flamenco music, and in dance bands and pop groups. In the latter the sound is amplified by electrical equipment and the strings are often plucked by a small piece of wood or metal called a plectrum.

4 Wind instruments

Wind instruments divide themselves into those made of wood (though nowadays some of the woodwind are made of metal) and those made of metal (the brass), but their basic material isn't the only difference.

Some of the woodwind are blown directly, some by means of a reed, but they are all tubes with side-holes that the player opens or closes, thus lengthening or shortening the vibrating column of air inside the tube. And the sound produced works on the principle that the shorter the tube, the higher the note.

The brass are blown by the players pressing their lips against a cup-shaped or funnel-shaped mouthpiece. The air vibrates inside the tube of the instrument, and the sound can be varied by blowing in such a way that instead of the whole tube vibrating, only part of it does. The tube can be made to vibrate in halves, quarters, and so on, but these proportions can't be altered and so at first brass players could only produce certain notes. This meant that they couldn't play an ordinary scale but, as we shall see, in time they managed to overcome this difficulty.

A problem that occurs with both woodwind and brass instruments is that on paper they seem to play in a different key from the rest of the orchestra. If you look at an orchestral score, you will see that the parts for the clarinet, the horn, and the trumpet are written in one key, and yet when they play, their music sounds in another key.

This is because they are transposing instruments, and although it sounds complicated, the reason why their music is written in a different key from that of the rest of the orchestra is that it makes life easier for the players. Take the clarinet, for example. The natural scale of the length of tube that produces the best sound for the clarinet is A or B flat, and so most clarinets are made in one or other of these keys. The player will have both instruments by him, and some passages will be easier to play on one, some on the other, so he will read the music in whichever key suits him best. The simplest key to play on a transposing instrument is always the key in which it is pitched, just as C major is the simplest key on the piano because it doesn't have any sharps or flats. So what the player of a transposing instrument gains is more simple fingering for certain notes.

The flute, recorder and piccolo

If you've heard James Galway playing, you'll know why the flute has been called the most perfect wind instrument. It is very nimble, at its best in very quick passages, and has a sparkling brilliant voice which can leap up to three octaves above middle C.

The flute is one of the oldest instruments and was played by the early Egyptians and the Greeks, though their flutes were not like those used today. The earliest flutes were held upright and the player put the end in his mouth, whereas today the flute is held crossways and blown sideways, so that the player directs air into it through his lips.

At the beginning of the Middle Ages all flutes were end-

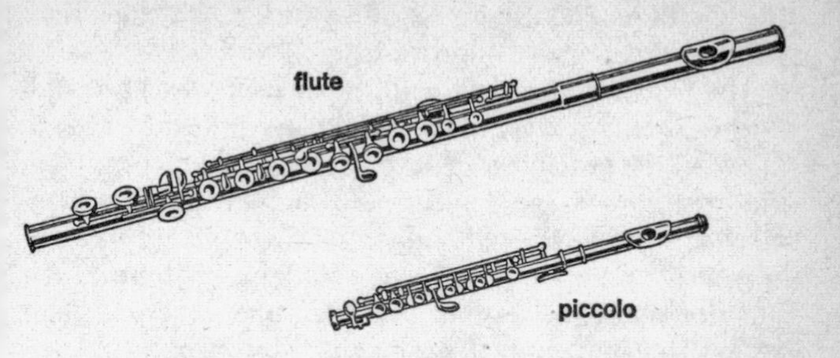

A flute and a piccolo

blown, and it wasn't until the twelfth century that the transverse flute appeared, and then it was usually played by soldiers. The end-blown flute, which we know better under the name recorder, remained the more important of the two until the eighteenth century. It was used by Purcell, Bach and Handel, who made it quite clear when they wanted the transverse flute instead. Bach asks for one by name in his *Brandenburg Concerto No. 5*, but *No. 4* should properly be played by recorders, though flutes are often used today.

The earliest recorders were made in one piece and in several sizes. A group, or consort as it was called, of recorders would include a treble, a tenor and a bass, and if there was an alto part, it was played by the soprano or tenor. Halfway through the seventeenth century the recorder was redesigned, so that now it was made in three parts that screwed together, and it began to be called the English flute to distinguish it from the German transverse flute.

The greatest flute player of Bach's day was Johann Quantz, who taught Frederick the Great to play the flute, wrote a guide to flute-playing, and composed about three hundred flute concertos. His flute had a mechanical device that opened and closed the bottom finger-hole, but this didn't extend the flute's range very much, and great efforts were made to improve it.

The man who finally found the answer was Theobald Boehm, an instrument maker who played the flute and so knew all the problems. He improved its tone by changing the position of the finger-holes, and invented a key-mechanism that opened and closed them. Older players, however, were reluctant to use his flute, in spite of its superior sound, because it meant learning a new system of fingering, but gradually they were won over.

Boehm's design is still used today, and the flute has changed little since his time. But although many British players still prefer a flute made of wood, most foreign flutes are made of metal, usually silver.

Meanwhile the recorder had been almost forgotten until by chance Arnold Dolmetsch, whom we last met reviving the lute, bought an old recorder at a sale in 1905. He taught himself to play it, and then he taught his children, who also had to learn all sorts of other old instruments so that the family could give concerts together.

Some years later, his youngest son Carl left the precious recorder on the platform at Waterloo Station, and as it was never found, Dolmetsch was forced to start making his own recorders. His lectures and concerts made many people aware of the charm of early music and of how easy some of the instruments were to play, especially the recorder. It became very popular with amateurs, who wanted the pleasure of playing simple but interesting music that didn't need too much practising or technique. If you've had the chance to play the recorder at school, you'll know how easy it is, though it would take a lot of practice to be a virtuoso player, like Carl Dolmetsch.

The flute was the first woodwind instrument to be a regular member of the orchestra, and it sounds well with the violins, the rest of the woodwind, and the horns. It turns up in concertos by Bach, Vivaldi, Pergolesi, and other Baroque composers, and although Mozart was said to dislike the flute, he wrote a delightful concerto for flute and harp. James Galway has also made a flute recording of Mozart's *Clarinet Concerto*, and the fast movement gains from the flute's agility. You can hear the flute doing a dance of its own in Tchaikovsky's *Nutcracker Suite*, and there is a haunting flute solo at the beginning of Debussy's *L'Après-midi d'un faune*.

Most orchestras have two flutes, and the second flautist also plays a smaller version of the flute called a piccolo. It has the highest voice in the orchestra, and despite its size it is so penetrating that it can be heard above everyone else. The piccolo is used for brilliant effects, and Beethoven was one of the first composers to introduce it into a symphony.

James Galway played with one of the greatest orchestras in the world, the Berlin Philharmonic, before he left to become a popular soloist who has made millions of people aware of the flute. If you're a convert, listen also to Richard Adeney and Jean-Pierre Rampal.

The oboe and cor anglais

There's a chance to pick out the sound of the oboe at the beginning of every concert, because it provides the note, an A, to which all the other players tune their instruments.

The sound comes in the first place from two thin pieces of reed in the mouthpiece which vibrate against each other when the player blows. The vibrating air is contained in a slender wooden tube, and the different notes are produced by a complicated arrangement of side-holes and keys. The oboe's range is about two and a half octaves, starting from the B flat below middle C.

The word 'oboe' comes from the French *hautbois* (high

wood), and *haut* was probably used in the sense of strong and loud rather than high-pitched. The early double-reed instruments were known as shawms, and the hautbois was a particular one used in France in the seventeenth century. The modern oboe is a descendant of this.

At first it was a loud rather coarse instrument best suited to outdoor music, but its tone gradually became more refined until it was at home in the graceful concertos of such composers as Vivaldi, Albinoni, Cimarosa, and Telemann. Haydn wrote music for it and so did

An oboe and a cor anglais with (right) a reed shown much enlarged

Mozart, and its plaintive voice was ideal for rather wistful melancholy tunes. Later it was to have some lovely solos in the symphonies of Beethoven and Schubert.

The most famous oboist of recent times is Leon Goossens, who made his name as a soloist (he inspired concertos by Richard Strauss and Vaughan Williams) and as a teacher who passed on his beautiful delicate sound to his pupils. Present-day players to look out for, especially on records, are Evelyn Rothwell and Heinz Holliger.

The cor anglais or English horn isn't a horn at all but an oboe with a deeper voice. It's longer than the oboe (remember, the longer the tube, the lower the note) and ends in a bulb-shaped bell, and it may once have been thought of as a horn because of its bent mouthpiece. It's a transposing instrument and plays a fifth lower than the key in which its music is written.

The cor anglais didn't join the orchestra until the end of the nineteenth century, when its deep mournful voice attracted the Romantic composers. Listen for it in the slow movement of Dvorak's *New World* symphony.

The clarinet

If you know Mozart's *Clarinet Concerto* or his equally beautiful *Quintet for Clarinet and Strings*, you won't need telling that the clarinet is a wonderfully expressive instrument. It can sing sweetly and brilliantly, run up and down with great agility, and if necessary be played so softly that it can truly be said to whisper.

The clarinet is usually made of wood or ebonite (a synthetic imitation of the black wood ebony), and is a long tube that flares out into a bell shape. The single reed that produces the sound is inside the mouthpiece, and you can't see it as you can the double reed of the oboe. The notes are produced by side-holes and keys, and a modern instrument will have at least twenty-four holes and seventeen keys.

Clarinets come in different sizes and the length determines their key. The most popular keys are B flat and A, but there's also the tiny clarinetto piccolo in E flat and the bass clarinet that is so long it turns up at the end. The clarinet is a transposing instrument and has a range of more than three octaves, the B flat starting from the D below middle C and the A a semitone lower.

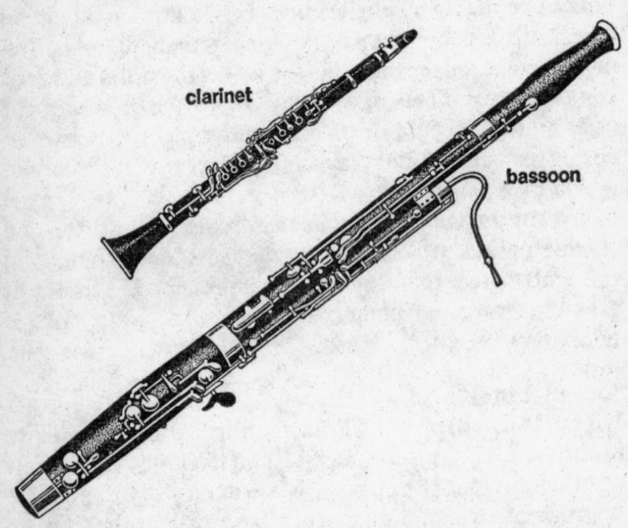

A clarinet and a bassoon

The modern clarinet was invented at the beginning of the eighteenth century by a German flute-maker, Johann Christoph Denner, who was fascinated by woodwind instruments and devised the clarinet as an improved version of a much older instrument, the *chalumeau*. The word is still used today to describe the distinctive dark notes of the clarinet's lowest octave.

At first the clarinet wasn't much liked. Its tone and

agility were thought inferior to the flute and the oboe, and so few players were prepared to spend time mastering it. The first musicians to realise its potential were a group of composers and players at the court of Mannheim in Germany, and their playing so impressed Mozart that the clarinet became his favourite wind instrument.

Mozart was a close friend of the brilliant Viennese clarinet player Anton Stadler, who was a member of the court wind band. His playing and that of his brother, who was also a clarinettist, inspired Mozart to write clarinet parts for many of his operas, symphonies, and concertos. Stadler invented a special clarinet capable of playing lower notes than usual, and Mozart wrote the quintet and the concerto – which was to be his last concerto – to show off Stadler's talent.

Although both pieces are justly popular today, they have only become so fairly recently, helped perhaps by the records of Jack Brymer and Gervase de Peyer, two of the world's best players. At the time, however, the two pieces were not so highly regarded, though Mozart certainly secured the clarinet an undisputed place in orchestral and chamber music.

By the nineteenth century the clarinet was to be found in most orchestras and military bands and had even made its way into church. Virtuoso players helped to make it more popular and impressed such composers as Weber, Brahms, and Wagner, but in time it was pushed aside by the much greater popularity of the piano and the violin. However it has made a comeback in the last fifty years, perhaps because its voice is so well suited to broadcasting and records.

It also adapts itself well to jazz music, and famous players include Benny Goodman and Artie Shaw.

The bassoon

Its rich deep voice makes the bassoon the 'cello' of the woodwind section, and the double bassoon, which plays an octave lower, is the woodwind equivalent of the double-bass.

It has been called the clown of the orchestra, and a good example of the bassoon in light-hearted mood is the amusing little tune it plays in Paul Dukas' *The Sorcerer's Apprentice*, the story in music of an apprentice who dabbles in magic and then finds that he can't call a halt to the spell. But the bassoon can be melancholy and sad, as in Tchaikovsky's *Pathétique* symphony, where it plays some very gloomy low notes.

There's no mistaking the bassoon's striking appearance: its tube is so long that it bends round and then rears up above the player's head. It's a member of the oboe family, and like it produces its sound from a double reed. As with the oboe, the player has to choose his reeds very carefully and take great care of them, and they often need to be scraped and adjusted at the last minute. The bassoon has a range of about three and a half octaves, starting from the B flat below the bass stave.

When the bassoon first appeared on the scene, in the sixteenth century, it was called a *curtal*, and it wasn't transformed into a bassoon until the eighteenth century. At first it was given the humble job of sharing the bass line with the cello and double-bass, but its distinctive sound was gradually recognised, especially by Mozart, who was very fond of wind instruments and wrote the bassoon a concerto of its own with a particularly lovely solo in the slow movement.

In time composers found that the bassoon went well with the horns at the top of its range and with the trombones at the bottom, and many of them including Beethoven and Tchaikovsky used it in their symphonies.

Stravinsky is a great bugbear for bassoon-players because his *Rite of Spring* opens with a fiendishly difficult solo.

Audiences are much more aware of the bassoon these days, helped by records and the outstanding playing of Archie Camden, the most famous British bassoonist.

The saxophone

You don't often see a saxophone in a symphony orchestra, but it's a popular member of military bands and dance bands and a superb jazz instrument.

It gets its name from Adolphe Sax, the man who invented it in 1846, and he seems to have been looking for an instrument that would be suitable for military bands and provide a link between the woodwind and brass sections. The saxophone has something in common with both, because its body is made of metal and its mouthpiece has a reed like a clarinet's. It comes in several sizes – the most common are the alto in E flat and the tenor in B flat – and its tube is usually doubled back on itself with note-holes controlled by a key system. Its range is about two and a half octaves.

Sax was right about the military bands, who soon adopted it, but the saxophone also appealed to the French composers Meyerbeer, Bizet, and Massenet, who gave it solo passages in their operas. Another composer who liked it was Richard Strauss, who had a quartet of saxophones in his *Domestic Symphony* and then had great difficulty finding any players. Wagner, however, was not won over and refused to have any saxophones in his work.

The stirring marches of Sousa helped to make the saxophone popular in America, but unlike the other band instruments it wasn't used for jazz until the 1920s. Then it spoke up loud and clear in the hands of Sidney Bechet,

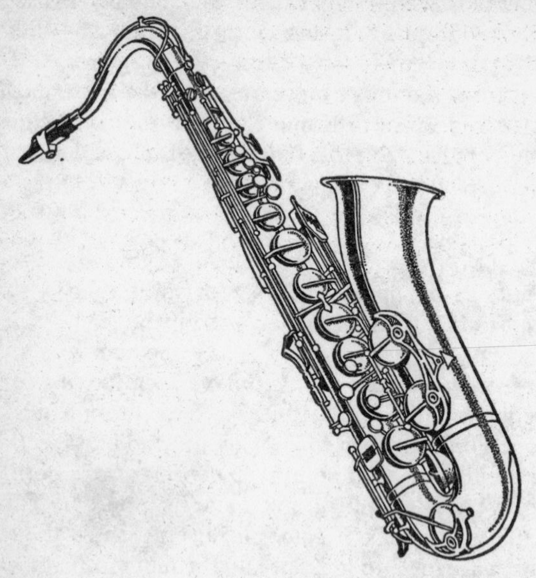

A tenor saxophone

Coleman Hawkins, Ben Webster, and more recently Charlie Parker, Stan Getz and the British player Johnny Dankworth.

The horn

The horn came to the orchestra from the hunting-field, where it had long been used to summon riders and hounds. It was introduced into opera and ballet music at the end of the seventeenth century, and it is still properly called the 'French' horn because it was in France that it acquired its distinctive coils, which make it easier to hold, and the bell-shaped end that enlarges its sound.

The early horns were not popular with other players

because they were loud and coarse, and their usefulness was limited by the fact that they could only play certain notes. In time ways round this were discovered, but they were clumsy. For example, a horn player at the Court of Dresden found that he could soften the tone of his instrument by putting his hand into the bell, and this also altered the pitch of his instrument and gave him a few extra notes. It was also possible to change key by lengthening the tube of the horn with extensions called crooks, but this meant the players carrying round up to nine extra pieces of tubing, and changing them over took time.

So it was a great step forward when a valve system was invented in the middle of the nineteenth century. Three extra pieces of tubing were welded on to the horn, and instead of having to change crooks the player could open up or shut off the extra tubing simply by pressing a valve. The modern horn is a transposing instrument in F, with three valves that give the player a range of three and a half octaves starting from the B below the bass staff. There are usually four horns in a symphony orchestra (though Wagner and later composers often use more), and to make life easier the first and third players concentrate on the high notes and the second and fourth on the lower.

The popularity of the horn today is due largely to the playing of one man, Dennis Brain, who was such a brilliant artist that he was able to draw attention to the horn and establish it as a solo instrument.

He came from a family of horn-players. His grandfather, father and two uncles were all fine players, and Dennis had his first blow at the horn when he was only three, though he didn't learn properly until he was in his teens. He was lucky to inherit the right kind of jaw for horn-playing, and he also had strong lip muscles and could keep up enormous air-pressure for long periods. He

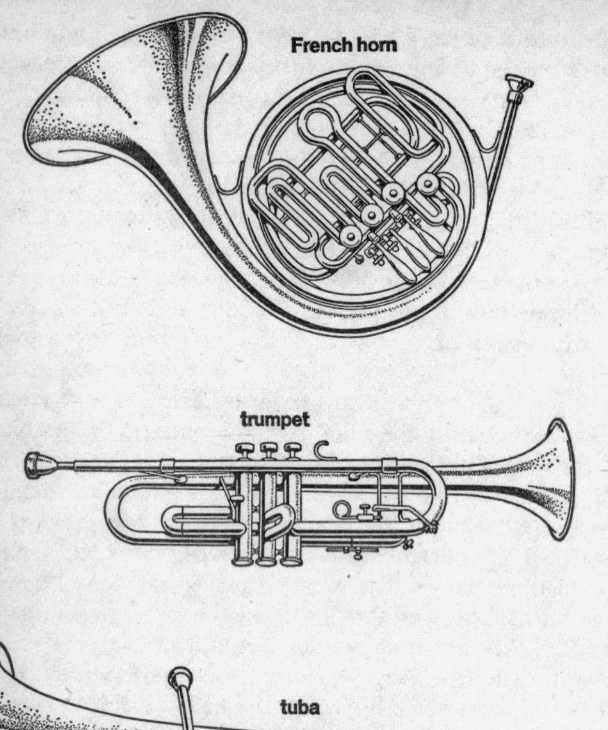

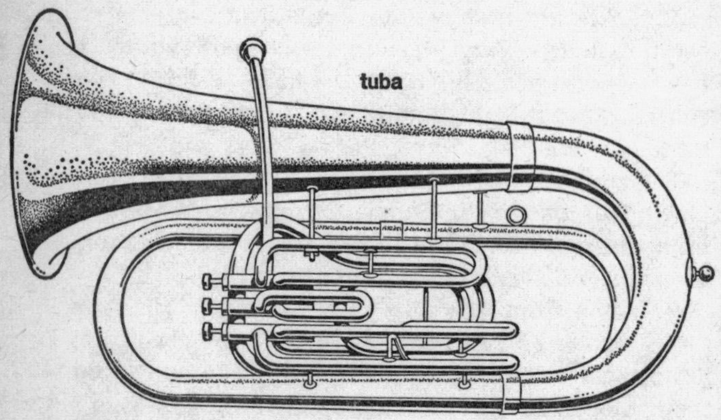

Brass instruments. The sackbut, on the right, was the trombone's ancestor

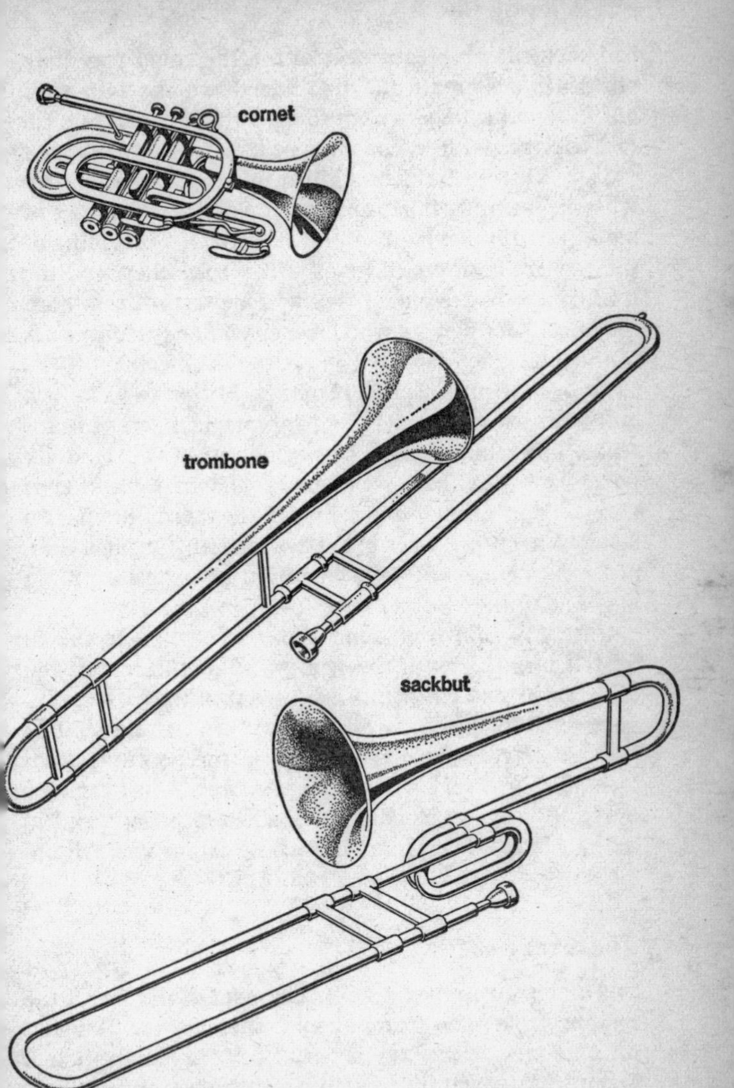
cornet
trombone
sackbut

had such superb breath control that he could play long phrases in one breath and didn't need to make unmusical breaks, and his fingers were so agile that he could tackle fast passages with legendary speed.

Sadly Dennis Brain was killed in a car crash in 1957 when he was only thirty-six, but you can get some idea of his wonderful playing from his records. His recording of the Mozart horn concertos is still a best-seller, and the four concertos are one of the supreme tests of solo horn playing. Other players who have given fine performances of them include Alan Civil and Barry Tuckwell.

Brain's artistry inspired Benjamin Britten to write several works for him including the magical *Serenade* for tenor, horn and strings. This winds its way round six poems, most of them well-known, and begins and ends with a gentle haunting solo for the horn. Brain also inspired a horn concerto by the modern German composer Paul Hindemith, who wrote it after hearing Brain play one of the Mozart concertos.

Once you know the sound of the horn you'll be able to hear it blending with the woodwind or the rest of the brass, or in solo passages. Listen for it in the slow movement of Tchaikovsky's *Fifth Symphony*, at the end of Dvorak's *New World* symphony, in the nocturne from Mendelssohn's *Midsummer Night's Dream*, in Wagner's operas (there's a splendid horn-call in *Siegfried*), and in the music of Richard Strauss, whose father was a horn-player.

The trumpet

One of the most rousing and triumphant of all tunes is the trumpet solo 'The trumpet shall sound' from Handel's *Messiah*, and if the trumpet really does herald the final Day of Judgement it's hard to imagine a better tune for it to play.

The earliest trumpets came in different sizes and could only play the notes belonging to their particular length, but in time, as with the horn, a valve system was developed that made it possible to vary the length of the coiled tubing by opening up extra parts of it, and so the trumpet too could change key without using crooks. The modern trumpet has three valves and a range of nearly three octaves. It is a transposing instrument, pitched in B flat or A, but there is also a trumpet in C which doesn't need to transpose its music.

The trumpet has always been good at making announcements. Its voice is penetrating, even shrill, and it can shout louder than any orchestra. In its early days, the natural trumpet (one without valves) was used to proclaim kings and victories, or to sound the alarm, and on the battlefield and at ceremonial occasions it was usually accompanied by drums. Its official duties are still carried out by the trumpeters of the Household Cavalry, who sound splendid fanfares on state occasions.

The trumpet is the soprano of the brass section, and at the time of Bach and Handel composers wrote chiefly for the top notes of the instrument and players perfected a special way of playing them known as the 'clarino technique'. An example of this kind of writing is the brilliant, very difficult trumpet part in the second of Bach's *Brandenburg Concertos*. Clarino playing gradually died out, partly because it required a great deal of practice, and nowadays players use a special trumpet in F to cope with these very high pieces.

Players were naturally anxious to improve the range and flexibility of their instrument, and Anton Weidinger, a famous trumpeter at the Viennese court, invented a trumpet with keys that could play far more notes. His achievement was celebrated by Haydn in his well-known *Trumpet Concerto*, which shows off the full glory of the new trumpet in its lively finale (the player to hear tackling this today is John Wilbraham). Weidinger's trumpet wasn't a lasting success, however, as it was soon overtaken by the vastly superior valved trumpet.

The trumpet always makes music more brilliant and exciting, and it excels at thrilling announcements such as the famous trumpet call which sounds at the most exciting moment of Beethoven's opera *Fidelio*. The best-known overture to this work (*Leonora*, No. 3), which is now played as a concert piece and not before the opera, has a wonderful fanfare that is all the more startling because it is usually played from elsewhere in the concert hall, such as the gallery.

The cornet is a poor relation of the trumpet and was popular before the valved trumpet was invented. You won't often see it in a symphony orchestra, but it is still a vital member of brass and military bands.

The great jazz trumpeter Louis Armstrong started off as a cornet player but switched over to the trumpet in the 1920s. The trumpet was ideal for jazz because it could laugh and cry and shout in exultation, and it expressed a whole new range of feeling in the hands of Armstrong, Bix Beiderbecke, Dizzy Gillespie, and Miles Davis.

The trombone

Its name, in Italian, means 'big trumpet', and this is really what it is, with more tubing and therefore a lower voice. You can easily recognise the trombones in an orchestra by the way the players lengthen or shorten their instruments by means of a slide which can make a difference of several feet. The slide mechanism has seven positions, and each one lowers the fundamental note by a semitone, so the slide does the same job as the valves of the horn and trumpet.

The player has to judge the correct position of the slide by ear, and it takes a lot of skill and practice to be able to slide smoothly from one note to the next.

Trombones first appeared in the fifteenth century and unlike most instruments they haven't changed much since then, though in those days they were called sackbuts.

There are usually three trombones in a symphony orchestra – two tenors and a bass, with a range of about two and a half octaves – but they didn't join the orchestra until late in the eighteenth century. Before that, they took part in festivities such as weddings and dances, and were the first wind instruments to be played in church. They were used by Gluck and Mozart in their operas, but they didn't really come into their own until they were needed in military bands, which were reorganised at the beginning of the nineteenth century, and in Italian romantic operas. Beethoven brought them into the symphony orchestra by including their rich powerful voices in his Fifth, Sixth and Ninth symphonies, and Wagner with his fondness for brass made good use of them.

The trombone was a jazz instrument from the early days of the Negro marching bands, and famous players include J. J. Johnson, Jack Teagarden, and Tommy Dorsey.

The tuba

When asked to describe what the tuba sounds like one tuba player said, '. . . the tuba can be a very savage, loud, strong instrument, but most of the time it provides a big sumptuous velvet cushion for the brass section to sit on.'

The tuba provides the bass voice of the brass, and it's a large instrument with coils of tubing ending in an enormous bell. It is descended from the serpent and the ophicleide, and it joined the orchestra in the middle of the nineteenth century when music was beginning to need a more powerful wind bass than the double bassoon. The first composer to use the tuba in a symphony orchestra was Berlioz, who included two tubas in his *Symphonie fantastique*. The tubas used in military bands are usually larger than the orchestral one, which is in F and has a range of about three octaves.

Although Vaughan Williams wrote a concerto for the tuba, it isn't really a solo instrument but intended to underline the bass notes of the brass. Wagner and Richard Strauss both used the tuba very effectively, and Wagner had special tubas made for his opera cycle *The Ring* because he wanted a tone colour that was midway between the horns and the bass tubas.

The background role of the tuba was illustrated some years ago by a popular record called 'Tubby the Tuba'. It was the story of a sad little instrument who never had a tune of his own to play. But one day Tubby does find a tune, and one by one all the other members of the orchestra ask him if they can play it too, until they build up to a splendid finale. If you ever come across the record, you'll find it hard to forget the plight of the tuba.

5 *Timpani, percussion and visitors to the orchestra*

Now we come to the more unusual, exciting-looking instruments that look as though they would be great fun to play. Most of them are either struck or shaken, and though this may look easy, if you bang the drum or clash the cymbals at the wrong moment, there's no hiding your mistake.

Easy to spot are the timpani or kettle-drums, heavy basins made of copper with a piece of calf-skin stretched tightly across the top and held firmly in place by a metal ring with adjustable screws. The screws are used to tune the drum, and you often see the timpanist (the official name for the drummer) tap the skin lightly, bend down to listen so closely that his face almost rests on the drum, and then adjust the screws. He is making sure that the drum is absolutely in tune, and he may need to check again during a work as well as at the beginning. It's a tricky business and nowadays can be done more quickly with a foot-pedal, but most players think the old way gives the best results.

If you watch carefully, you'll see that the timpanist has several pairs of drumsticks. They have felt heads, some harder than others, and he uses them to produce sounds that range from a tremendous crash to quiet taps or a muffled roll.

Orchestral drums. Left to right: bass drum, a pair of kettledrums or timpani and a snare drum

The kettle-drum is the king of the percussion, but it's not the only drum on the scene. The bass drum – the big drum you see in a marching band – stands on its side and gives a low boom when struck. The much smaller side drum – called 'side' because in military bands it is slung round the neck on a strap and hangs down one side – is played with wooden sticks. It has wire strings called 'snares' across the bottom, and these make an impressive rattle. The side drum is used for a fast roll and to emphasise the beat of a strong rhythm. Look out for the kettle-drum and side drum in Handel's *Music for the Royal Fireworks,* written by order of George II to be played at a splendid firework display held in the Green Park in 1749.

The triangle and the cymbals came originally from Turkish military bands and made their first appearance in opera. The triangle is made of steel and struck with a special steel beater, and its only real solo comes in Liszt's *First Piano Concerto.* The cymbals are thin shallow brass plates that are either crashed together or hung up and hit with a stick to produce a sinister roll.

The tambourine is hung with tiny metal plates that jingle when it is struck or shaken, and the castanets are a pair of wooden shells clapped together to make a distinctive clicking sound. They are sometimes used to accompany dances and suggest a gipsy or Spanish setting.

Other occasional visitors include three struck with hammers. The tubular bells are a row of metal tubes of different lengths used to imitate a peal of bells. The glockenspiel is a row of small steel plates that give a sparkling silvery sound when struck, and the xylophone is a similar arrangement made of wood, which sounds more like a dry rattle.

Modern music in particular has made some strange demands on the percussion. All sorts of odd things have been used, from rattles and sirens to a machine for imitat-

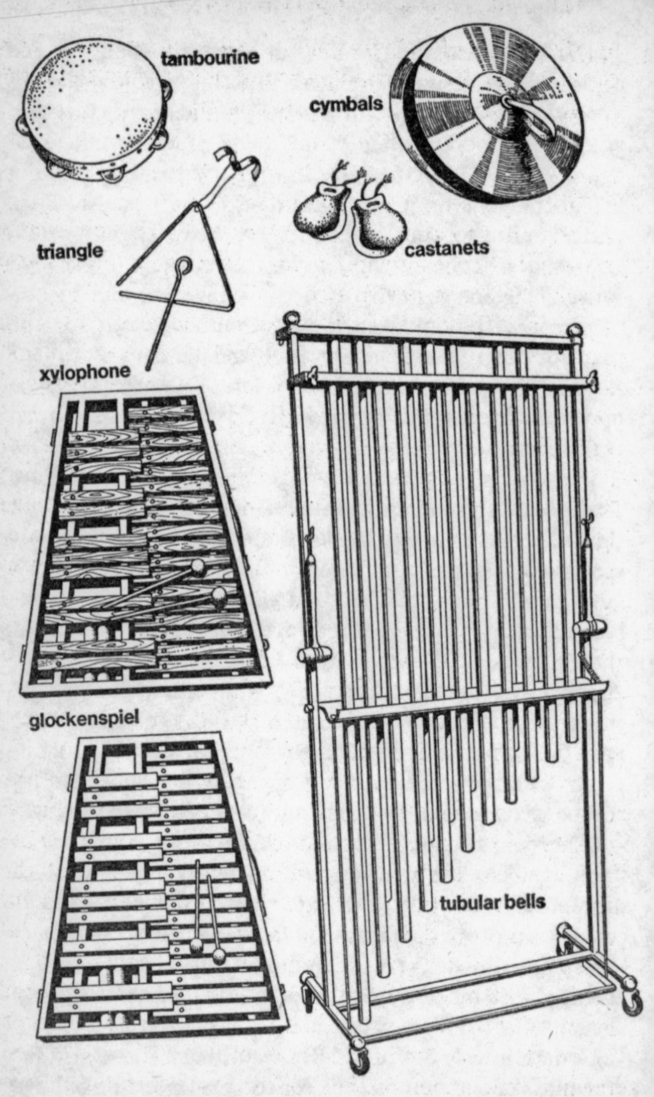

Orchestral percussion

ing the sound of the wind, and the French composer Erik Satie asked for the menacing sound of gunshots and typewriters in his music for the ballet *Parade*.

The harp

Angels are supposed to play harps and although there's no way of being sure about this, the harp certainly has a very ancient and distinguished history.

The ancient Egyptians had harps, and wall paintings, carvings, and the drawings in those old manuscripts so splendidly illustrated by the monks give a good idea of what these early harps looked like.

The most famous old harp still in existence is the Brian Boru harp which may have belonged to an Irish High King who was killed in 1014. It is small enough to have been carried around quite easily, and the travelling minstrel with his extra long fingernails – specially grown to pluck the metal strings – was a familiar sight in Ireland for centuries. He would travel round from one country house to the next to entertain the landed gentry, and they usually paid for his training. The importance of the harp in Ireland is commemorated in the Royal Arms, where Northern Ireland is represented by a harp.

Small harps were fine for accompanying songs, but like other instruments the harp couldn't make much musical progress until it was possible to change key more easily. The answer didn't turn up until nearly the end of the seventeenth century, but once the pedal harp was invented it gave the player a new freedom. The pedal mechanism was taken a stage further by a brilliant instrument-maker called Sebastian Erard, who introduced what he called the double-action harp. This made it possible to play in all the major and minor keys, and it transformed the harp into an instrument for serious musicians.

It also changed its shape and size and turned it into an

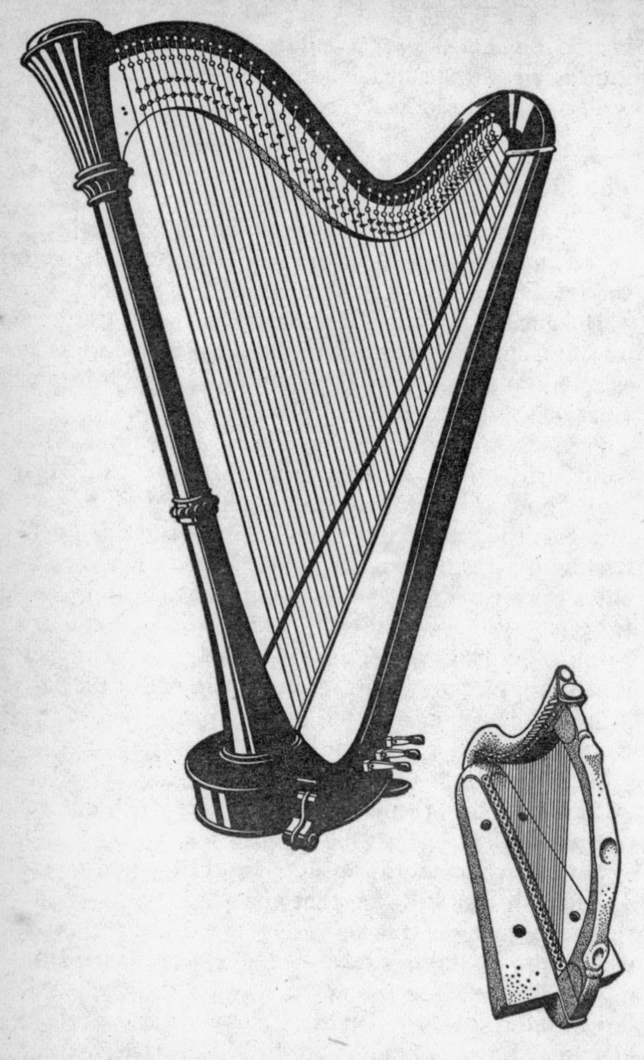

A modern orchestral harp (left) and an Irish harp from the fifteenth century

impressive giant. The concert harp of today is about six feet tall and has forty-seven strings of different lengths that run from tuning pegs at the top of the frame down to a hollow box at the bottom which increases the sound. The harp's neck is curved to give all the strings an even tension, and the longest strings are furthest away from the player. The strings are sounded by plucking them, and the player changes key with the help of seven pedals which are moved by the feet. The harp has a range of six and a half octaves, and all the strings have to be tuned separately, which is why the harpist always arrives on the platform well before the other players.

The harp makes such a distinctive sound that it stands out quite clearly from the other instruments. Listen out for its *arpeggios*, when it plays the notes of a chord one after the other, and its *glissando*, a graceful tinkling slide up and down the scale.

The pedal harp was very popular at the French court during the eighteenth century, and it was one instrument that was proper for ladies to play. One Frenchwoman, Madame de Genlis, made her fortune playing the harp – though she had to work very hard at it. She claimed to practise as much as twelve hours a day at the age of fifteen, but it seems to have been worth her while because she was often able to pay for her dinner by entertaining the other guests, and her playing also brought her a rich husband. She became a governess to the French royal family and played to the ill-fated queen Marie Antoinette, who took lessons herself.

Many other young ladies shared her taste, and when Mozart was in Paris he gave lessons in composition to the Duc de Guines' daughter, who was *magnifique* at the harp. Sadly the poor girl wasn't *magnifique* at composition, and Mozart was soon calling her stupid and lazy. But there was one happy outcome: he wrote a charming double concerto for her and her father, who was a brilliant flute player. Mozart didn't like the flute or the harp much, but he may have been prejudiced by the fact that he wasn't paid much for this concerto.

The double-action harp soon produced a number of virtuoso players, but it proved too difficult for most amateurs. Although it had been the fashion for ladies to accompany any gentlemen who sang or played the flute, they now turned their attention to a new instrument, the piano, which they found easier to manage.

But if the harp was driven out of the drawing room, it found far more music to play on the concert platform. Much of it was written by the harpists themselves, who began arranging and adapting the piano music of Chopin and Liszt. Most composers were slow to realise its new possibilities, but Berlioz was a great admirer of the great harpist Parish-Alvars, whom he called 'the Liszt of the harp'. He wrote parts for two harps in his *Symphonie fantastique* and called for ten harps in his dramatic cantata *The Damnation of Faust*.

Liszt had many harp parts in his orchestral music and his son-in-law, Richard Wagner, made splendid use of the harp in his operas including a passage at the beginning of *Das Rheingold* that was written for six harps, though most modern opera houses can't usually afford more than two.

The most famous harp solo comes in the 'Waltz of the Flowers' from Tchaikovsky's *Nutcracker Suite*, and you'll find the harp turning up in operas, ballets, tone poems, and symphonies.

Outstanding players of today include Nicanor Zabeleta, Maria Korchinska, and Osian Ellis.

The clavichord, harpsichord, and piano

The piano is one of the orchestra's grandest and most imposing guests, but surprisingly it was a fairly late arrival on the music scene.

It had of course a number of ancestors including the zither, the dulcimer, and the psaltery, but its most immediate predecessors were two instruments – the clavichord and the harpsichord – that are still played today, though only by specialist musicians.

The clavichord was most at home in the drawing room, and even there its soft tone could easily be drowned by conversation. Its strings are struck by small metal blades called tangents, and the notes can be made to vibrate, an effect that is not possible on other keyboard instruments.

It is most suited to short delicate pieces, and it was a favourite instrument of one of Bach's sons, C. P. E. Bach, whose playing was described by one listener as being so touching in slow movements that it sounded like 'a cry of sorrow and complaint'.

The clavichord went out of fashion because it was too quiet to hold its own against other instruments, but its rival, the harpsichord, had a more distinguished career.

Unlike the clavichord and the piano, the strings of the harpsichord are not struck by hammers but plucked mechanically by a plectrum. Like so many instruments, it was invented in Italy, but some of the most beautiful harpsichords were made at Antwerp in Belgium. They not only sounded exquisite but looked it too. Their keys were inlaid with tortoiseshell or mother-of-pearl, and their lids were often decorated with paintings by such famous artists as Van Dyck and Breughel. Fine harpsichords were also made in England, notably by two immigrants called Shudi and Kirkman.

During the seventeenth century the harpsichord was much used as a continuo instrument (see page 44), and its tinkling voice was clearly heard in trio sonatas, suites of dances, and concertos.

One of the greatest harpsichord players was the Italian composer Domenico Scarlatti, who wrote more than five

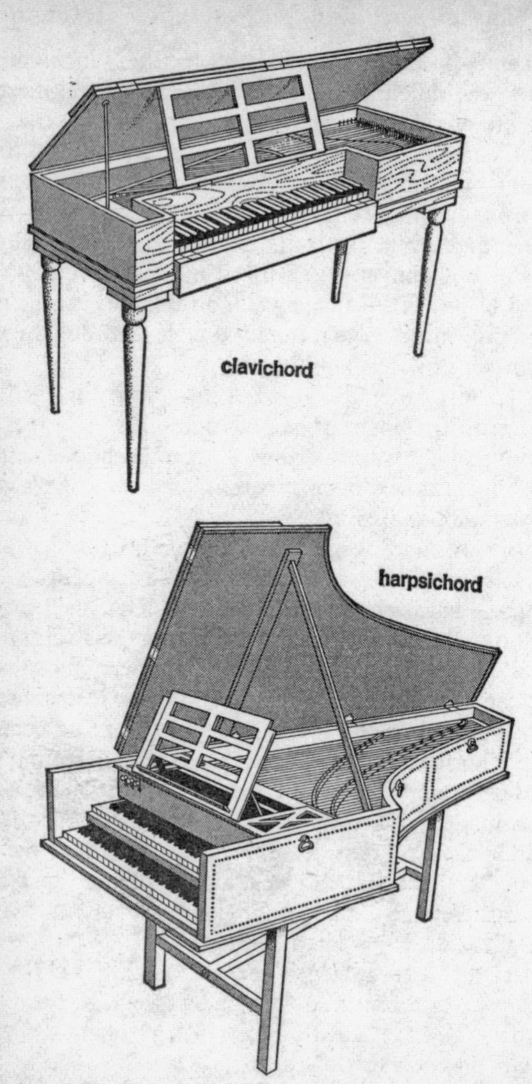

The clavichord and harpsichord were ancestors of the modern piano

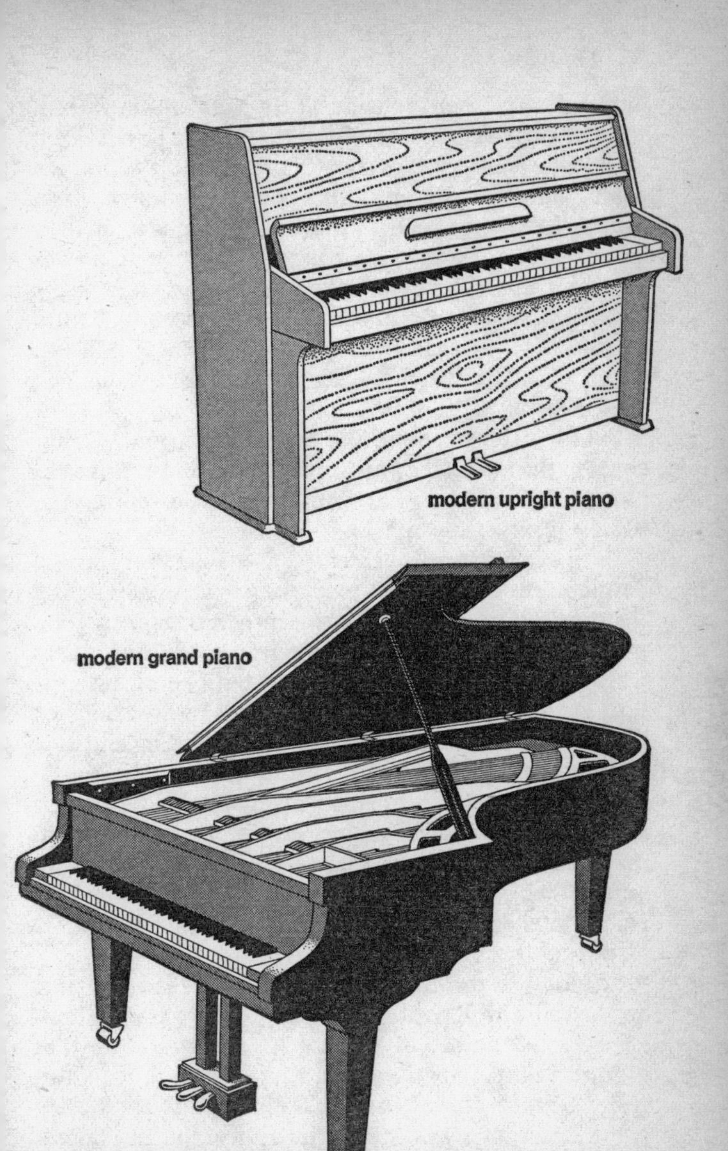
modern upright piano
modern grand piano

hundred harpsichord sonatas. These were one-movement sonatas, early versions of a form that was to be perfected by Beethoven. Scarlatti's sonatas are often played on the piano, but the American harpsichordist Ralph Kirkpatrick has done much to make them popular in their original form. Another great harpsichord composer was the Frenchman François Couperin. Many of his pieces have very strange titles and have recently been brilliantly recorded by the Canadian harpsichordist Kenneth Gilbert. Other players to watch out for are George Malcolm and Trevor Pinnock.

But for all its grace and charm the harpsichord was not equal to the new forces stirring in music, and it was to be replaced by an instrument whose very name – *fortepiano* – made plain its advantages.

Once again it was invented by an Italian, but the real development of the piano took place in Germany during the first half of the eighteenth century. The great composer Bach had shown little interest in the new piano when it was demonstrated to him, but one of his sons, J. C. Bach (known as the 'English Bach' because he lived in London), played the first piano solo in England at a concert given in 1786.

By then pianos were being made in England by a German immigrant called Zumpe, who started a workshop that made small square pianos. They were not really 'square' but oblong, and were forerunners of the upright piano, intended for the home rather than the concert platform.

London was one of the great centres of piano-making, and its only real rival was Vienna, where music flourished in the houses of the nobility. It was there that Mozart took part in a contest with Clementi, who also had the reputation of being a brilliant performer. They played their own works, sight-read some sonatas, improvised on a given theme, and although neither was a clear winner, it was generally agreed that Mozart's playing was more refined. He certainly had no doubt about this and was very rude about Clementi, saying that he had neither taste nor feeling.

Clementi returned to England, where he had been brought up, and became a successful piano-maker and salesman. His firm was second only to Broadwood, which had become the largest piano firm in the world, turning out more than eight thousand pianos in the last twenty years of the eighteenth century. They were now being produced at a price that more and more people could afford, and they soon became a kind of status symbol such as a car or a colour television is today.

Although Mozart's piano concertos give the soloist wonderful opportunities and are one of the summits of piano music, it was Beethoven who forced makers to improve the piano.

His demands were in part the result of a cruel handicap, his increasing deafness, which made him strike the keys with tremendous force in a desperate attempt to hear some sound from them, but even before this he was a forceful player with the reputation of being a piano destroyer. His sonatas and concertos made demands beyond the limits of the pianos of his time: he wanted more notes, he wanted a better sustaining pedal, and he wanted subtle differences of tone. His *Hammerklavier Sonata* unleashed a fury that needed a much stronger, more responsive instrument, and it spurred makers to new developments including the use of metal frames.

During the 1830s and '40s these improvements led to a new type of performer, the virtuoso pianist, who enjoyed the kind of reception we give to pop stars. Liszt, inspired by the example of the violinist Paganini, was a showman who attacked the piano with his whole being. He had a marvellous technique, he could make up music as he went along, and he could play a new concerto at sight.

After his concerts his admirers fought for souvenirs such as his gloves, pieces of his clothing, and fragments of the pianos he had destroyed as he thundered up and down the keys. But he was also a serious composer, as you can hear in his exciting *Hungarian Rhapsodies* and the great B minor sonata.

In contrast, Chopin was a much more delicate pianist, partly because he was never a strong man and was increasingly weakened by illness. His music expresses the dreamy, reflective side of the Romantics, and he encouraged the fashion for shorter pieces such as preludes, nocturnes, ballades, and those based on dances such as the waltz, polonaise, and mazurka.

If you like his music, you'll also enjoy that of his contemporary, Robert Schumann, who wrote an enchanting piano concerto and many imaginative and sensitive short pieces. These have been wonderfully interpreted by the great Russian pianist Sviatoslav Richter, who doesn't often play outside Russia but is justly famous through his recordings.

The development of the smaller upright had brought the piano into many more homes. During the Victorian period it took over from the guitar and the harp, and established itself as the ideal instrument for all the family. Playing became a desirable accomplishment, and the girls who struggled with their practising were comforted by the thought that they might well catch the eye of an eligible young man while seated at the piano.

Meanwhile the most famous makers wanted to be supreme on the concert platform. In America a young German founded the firm of Steinway and made grand pianos that were both loud and sensitive, while in Europe, Bechstein, Bluthner and Ibach competed against each other. As you've probably noticed, you can usually tell the make of piano being used at a concert because the makers aren't shy about seeing that their name is displayed in large letters.

The frenzy of the virtuoso players gave way to artists who didn't play their own works but were intent on interpreting those of the great composers, and in 1860 the complete cycle of Beethoven's thirty-two piano sonatas was played for the first time.

Interestingly, in those days players were criticised if they played from memory, because it was thought insulting to the composer to play his music without a score. But today most players are expected to know a work by heart, and even those who do use music could probably play without it.

In the twentieth century the romantic tradition was continued by Debussy, whose misty sound pictures are like paintings by the Impressionists, and Gabriel Fauré, whose beautiful nocturnes, barcarolles and impromptus deserve to be better known. But other composers, such as Bartok, Hindemith, Prokofiev, and Stravinsky, have seen the piano as a percussion instrument and exploited its hammers in harsh complex rhythms.

The piano has produced more fine soloists than any other instrument, and sadly there isn't room to mention more than a few. Outstanding players of today include Vladimir Ashkenazy, Daniel Barenboim, Alfred Brendel, Stephen Bishop-Kovacevitch, Radu Lupu, Murray Perahia, Maurizio Pollini, and the oldest and acknowledged master – still playing at over eighty – Artur Rubinstein.

Your favourite may depend in part on your favourite composer, for many pianists develop a special sympathy with certain composers. Records will also put you in touch with some of the great players of the past, such as Artur Schnabel, Alfred Cortot, and Dinu Lipatti, who died tragically young and made a famous recording of the Schumann and Grieg concertos. And if you want to spot future great players, look out for the winners of the

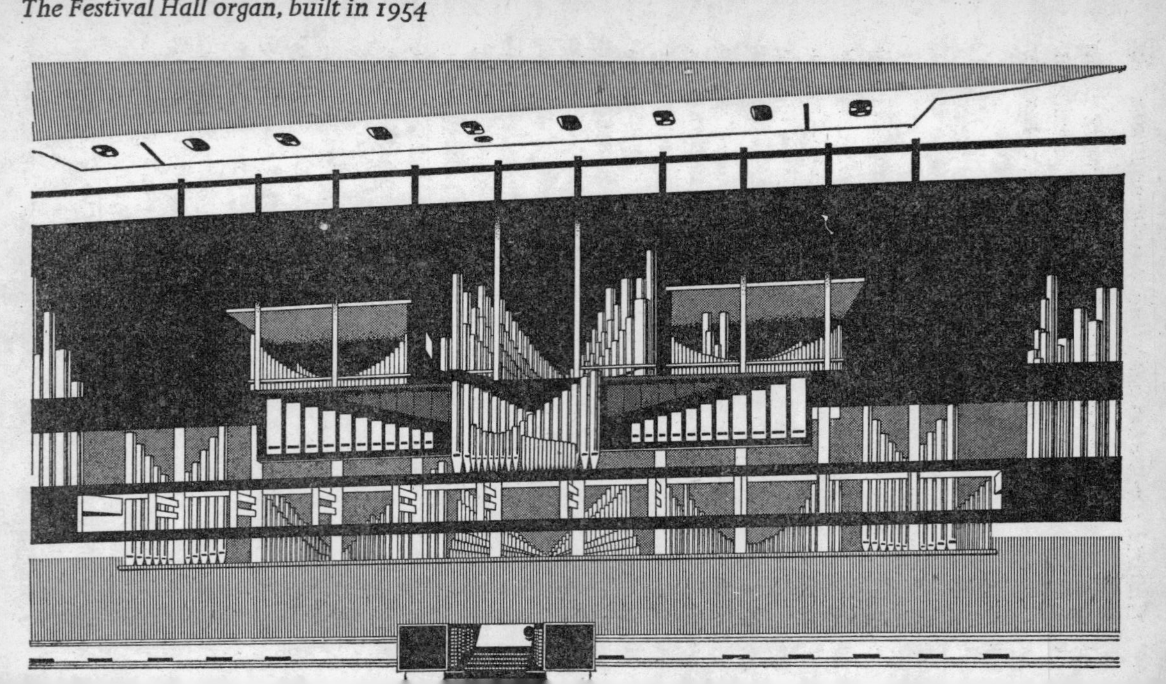

The Festival Hall organ, built in 1954

Leeds, Moscow Tchaikovsky, and Warsaw Chopin piano competitions. Andrei Gavrilov and Krystian Zimerman, two recent winners, have both been tipped as future star players.

The organ

You don't often hear the organ with an orchestra, except in choral works and in a rarity such as Saint-Saëns' *Third Symphony*, but the organ is one of the oldest instruments and a vital part of the great tradition of church music.

It is a wind instrument with several keyboards played by the hands and feet, and the basic principle on which it works – pipes filled with wind – was probably first suggested by the sound of the wind passing through broken reeds. Organs always have stacks of pipes, and in a big organ there may be three or more pipes to each note. The pipes are opened and closed by a system of stops, and the wind comes from a bellows that used to be worked by hand but is now usually powered by electricity. As organs became more complex, several of them were sometimes joined to form huge organs with up to five keyboards. The keyboards had expressive names such as Choir, Great, Swell, Solo, and Echo.

Until modern times organs were built to suit the special needs of their time, and so an organ right for the music of one composer may not be ideal for an earlier or later one.

Organ building and organ music developed together, and the summit was reached in the music of J. S. Bach. Bach spent most of his life as an organist and choirmaster, and he was so keen on the organ that he was prepared to walk over two hundred miles to visit his great predecessor Buxtehude.

Bach began by writing variations on his favourite

The tonal range of orchestral instruments

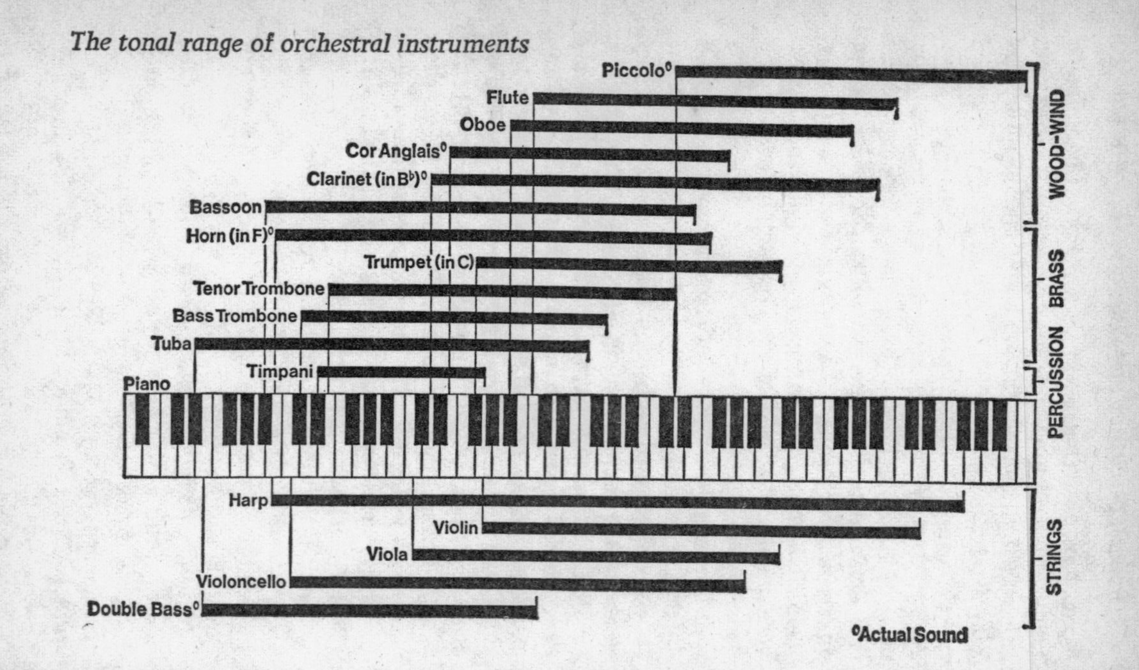

hymn tunes and then went on from these chorale preludes to more elaborate pieces such as the *Prelude and Fugue in D*, the *Toccata and Fugue in D minor* (his best-known organ work), the *Fantasia and Fugue in C minor* and the *Passaglia and Fugue in C minor*. These great organ showpieces were written during the years when he was the organist at Weimar, and his playing was so admired that he was often asked to give recitals in nearby cities. To sample the organ at its most magnificent, try to hear these pieces played by Helmut Walcha or Lionel Rogg, both famous performers of Bach's music.

Of course organ music didn't come to an end with Bach, but although Handel wrote some organ concertos, music as a whole began to move away from the church and the leading composers neglected the organ. But some fine organ music was written in the nineteenth century by Mendelssohn, Parry, Stanford, and the French composers César Franck and Charles Widor.

Recently there has been much more interest in the organ, and an important landmark was the building in 1954 of a superb and very beautiful-looking organ for the Royal Festival Hall.

6 The whole orchestra

The first musicians who formed themselves into groups to play together didn't perform in concert halls but in the palaces and great houses of kings and noblemen. They were often expected to play at mealtimes – especially when a great feast or special banquet was held – and you may have seen the minstrels' gallery where they sat in the great hall of a stately home. They played the viols and violins, lutes, recorders, sackbuts, and later hautboys and flutes, and provided airs to soothe and dances to entertain the company.

The musicians at court were also expected to play the trumpets and drums used to announce important visitors and celebrate victories, and as time went on the various princes and nobles of the courts of Europe – and in those days there were a lot of small states and dukedoms – vied with each other for the grandest and most skilful band of musicians. They also had their own composers who were required to write suitable music for the great occasions of the household, and a talented composer would be much in demand and also benefit from having a rich and powerful patron who was willing to spend his money freely on music.

One such composer was Joseph Haydn, who in 1761 signed a contract to become assistant *Kapellmeister* (or musical director) to Prince Paul Esterhazy. The Esterhazys were a noble Hungarian family who lived in a grand castle and of course had their own band of musicians. Prince Paul and his successor Prince Nicholas (for whom Haydn worked for twenty-eight years) were both very fond of music and played themselves. Prince Nicholas played a curious instrument called a baryton – described as a cross between a viol da gamba and a guitar – and Haydn went to the trouble of learning to play it so that he could please his employer by writing pieces for it.

He found himself in charge of a small orchestra of a dozen of so players and a choir of six. They had to perform symphonies, operas, serenades and quartets several times a week, and Haydn not only had to rehearse the players but make sure that their instruments were in order and that they all had their music – if necessary, he copied out any extra parts needed. He was also expected to compose whatever music the Prince wanted: requiem masses for anyone who died, dances, serenades and operas for weddings, pieces to celebrate the visit of important guests such as the Empress Maria Theresa, in whose honour Haydn wrote a symphony and two operas when she visited the Prince in 1773.

Haydn's position was in fact that of a superior servant. He and his fellow musicians wore a uniform and were expected to appear in clean linen with white stockings and to see that their hair was properly dressed in the style of the day, which meant powdering it and tying it back in a pigtail or a bag. He was given his orders every day, and had to make sure that the other players behaved themselves and were a credit to His Highness.

Today we would find it strange that a musician of Haydn's genius was happy to accept such conditions, but there is no evidence that Haydn himself felt degraded by them. He had known what it was to go hungry, and so he was delighted to have a post that brought him security and a pleasant home. He didn't see himself as a temperamental genius who could only write music when he felt in the mood. Rather, he was a craftsman with a practical job to do: writing and performing music that was an accepted part of everyday life. And unlike many composers today, he had the satisfaction of knowing that his music would be performed, and of knowing the musicians who were to play it. There were indeed many drawbacks to such a position, such as long hours, too much work, isolation from the rest of the musical world, but Haydn made up his mind to make the best of the advantages, which he summed up as:

> My prince was satisfied with all my works, I was praised, as head of an orchestra I could experiment, observe what heightened the effect and what weakened it, and so could improve, expand, cut, take risks, I was cut off from the world, there was no one near me to torment me or make me doubt myself, and so I had to become original. (Translated by Rosemary Hughes and quoted in her book *Haydn*)

The frustration Haydn and his fellows sometimes felt is well illustrated by his *Farewell* symphony. Every year the Prince liked to stay in a splendid new palace-cum-shooting lodge that he had built at Esterhazy. Although it had its own opera house and picture gallery, there wasn't much room for the musicians and none for their families. So before long they were longing to go home. Haydn was too diplomatic to ask the Prince when he was planning to leave, but he wrote a symphony which ended with the players finishing their parts one by one and then tiptoeing out, until there were only two violins left to play the final notes. Luckily the Prince was delighted with the piece – and got the message.

But if Haydn's music testifies to the good side of patronage, Mozart's experience of it was disastrous. He was not appreciated by his first employer, the Archbishop of Salzburg, for whom his father too worked, and he resented the restrictions and indignities of his position and struggled to gain his freedom. But he found little practical help for his genius, though it was certainly recognised at the time, and although he received some commissions, they were not enough to keep him and his family. When he died, worn out by disappointment and despair, there was not enough money to pay for a proper funeral, and his body was thrown into a communal grave alongside those of other paupers.

In England, however, music was being performed in rather different circumstances. Most of the aristocracy were not very interested in music, at least in their country houses, and instead they patronised it as part of the London season which began in the winter when they returned for the opening of Parliament and a round of theatrical and musical diversions.

The first concerts in the world at which people paid to listen had been staged in 1672 by John Bannister, a violinist in the King's band, and a few years later a series of concerts was organised by Thomas Britton, who started life selling coal from a handcart and made enough money to collect old music as a hobby. He kept his music in a loft above the stable where he stored the coal, and held concerts in the loft every Thursday night. In spite of such an uncomfortable setting – the room was very low and the only way in was up a dangerous flight of steps – Britton attracted a distinguished audience including the composer Handel, who sometimes played on a small organ.

Of course concert-giving soon became a commercial business, with concerts organised by professional promoters and music societies. Haydn was invited to England by a promoter who wanted to steal a march on his rivals, and was offered a fee of £300 for six symphonies. It is nice to know that London gave him a most enthusiastic reception. He was entertained by royalty, had his portrait painted, and was made a Doctor of Music by Oxford University.

Mozart had been greatly impressed by the superb band of musicians he heard at the court of the Elector Palatine at Mannheim, and they have a good claim to be the first real symphony orchestra. Thanks to their example, by the end of the eighteenth century the orchestra had become an organised band of string and woodwind players, and by the middle of the nineteenth century they had been joined by the brass and percussion and were recognisably the orchestra we know today.

But the standard of performance wasn't, and one of its sternest critics was the French composer Hector Berlioz, who gives a fascinating account of the kind of outrage composers had to put up with in his outspoken *Memoirs*. Berlioz was so dedicated to music that he often knew the score by heart and was furious at the changes made by the conductors and players of his time. On one occasion, when he was at a performance of an opera by Gluck, he became so angry at the liberties being taken by the conductor that he shouted out, 'There are no cymbals there ... Who has dared to correct Gluck? ... Why aren't the trombones playing?' The audience, who didn't know any better, were somewhat surprised by his outburst, but Berlioz had the satisfaction of hearing everything put right at later performances.

He was not the only composer to be dismayed by poor orchestral standards, and he, Wagner, Mahler and Richard Strauss all made such demands on players that they were forced to become more skilful. The nineteenth century saw the founding of some of the world's greatest orchestras – the Vienna Philharmonic and the New York Philharmonic in 1842, the Hallé Orchestra in 1858, the Boston Symphony in 1881, the Amsterdam Concertgebouw and the Berlin Philharmonic in 1882, the Chicago Symphony in 1886, the Cincinnati Symphony in

1893, the Pittsburgh Symphony in 1899 – and the opening of some famous concert-halls. In England there were concerts at the Crystal Palace, an exhibition hall of glass that looked like a giant greenhouse, at the Royal Albert Hall, opened in 1871 in memory of the Prince Consort, and at the Queen's Hall, which opened in 1893 and became the centre of London's music life until it was destroyed by a bomb in 1941.

The Queen's Hall was the home of the Promenade Concerts, which had started in 1895 with Sir Henry Wood as their guiding spirit and chief conductor. Sir Henry, who was a strict disciplinarian, was responsible for an orchestral revolution when he refused to allow players to use deputies. The deputy system was the result of the precarious conditions under which the players worked. They had no permanent contracts to tie them to one orchestra, and so if they were offered more money elsewhere, they would send along another player to take their place. By the day of the performance the conductor could find himself facing players he'd never seen before, and although they were often brilliant sight-readers – they had to be – the finer qualities that come from an orchestra rehearsing regularly were bound to be lacking. So no wonder Sir Henry put his foot down about deputies.

Half his players walked out and then set up their own independent company, the London Symphony Orchestra. They made their own rules, put on concerts themselves, and hired the top conductors and soloists. The idea worked, and the company was able to survive all sorts of storms including the arrival of radio, which threatened to make listening at home more popular than live concerts.

The London Symphony is still one of London's top orchestras and much of its money comes from records made with showbiz-personality André Previn, its former principal conductor. Together with the London Philharmonic, the Royal Philharmonic and the Philharmonia orchestras, it has helped to make London one of the great music centres of the world which attracts such outstanding conductors as Claudio Abbado, Karl Böhm, Colin Davis, Bernard Haitink, Lorin Maazel, Richardo Muti, and Sir Georg Solti, and even an occasional visit from the supreme maestro Herbert von Karajan.

The members of an orchestra probably all have their own ideas about music, but they have to put these on one side and play as a team. And it is the conductor's job to persuade them to follow his interpretation.

Today the conductor is an important, glamorous figure, often like Karajan (the highest-paid conductor in the world) the star turn of the orchestra, but this is a recent development. Originally the orchestra simply needed someone to beat time, and this might be done by the harpsichord player, a soloist, or perhaps the chief singer. Often the composer himself conducted – Haydn as a violinist, Mozart from the piano – and this worked very well when orchestras were still fairly small. Sometimes the orchestra was led by the chief violinist, and this is why he is still known as the leader and usually comes on by himself and gets a special round of applause.

The use of a stick or baton to conduct didn't happen until the nineteenth century, but earlier musicians sometimes used a stick or their hands to beat time. The French composer Lully used to thump on the floor with a stick. On one occasion he hit his foot by mistake and gave it such a hard blow that it caused an abscess from which he died.

As orchestras grew bigger and orchestral music became more complicated, it was obvious that someone was needed to take charge. One of the first conductors to use a baton was the German violinist and composer Louis Spohr, who is said to have introduced the idea to London in 1820. Certainly by about 1850 the conductor was firmly established and beginning to assert his personality. The French conductor Jullien insisted on wearing white gloves to

1 Grand opera — a scene from Verdi's Aida *at the Royal Opera House, Covent Garden, with soloists Grace Bumbry and Jon Vickers*

2 Benjamin Britten (left), one of Britain's best known modern composers, whose works include some highly original compositions for children as well as songs, operas and orchestral music

3 Pablo Casals (below, centre) was probably the greatest cellist of all time

4 The Japanese Suzuki method of teaching the violin (right) means that you can start playing early — at the age of two!

5 Part of a crowd of over 2000 Japanese child violinists (below) show what the Suzuki method can achieve

6 *Above: a great British musical occasion — the Last Night of the Proms*

7 *Below: young musicians — the National Youth Orchestra of Great Britain in rehearsal*

8 *Gary Bond (left) as Che Guevara in* Evita

9 *Elaine Page (below) as Eva Peron in* Evita

10 The brilliant flautist James Galway (right) has done much to revive popular interest in the flute

11 Julian Bream (below, left) and John Williams (below, right) have done more than anyone else to introduce audiences to the marvellous music written for the classical guitar

12 Composer and performers: Benjamin Britten rehearses the Jeney twins in the variations for flute, violin and piano which he wrote for them

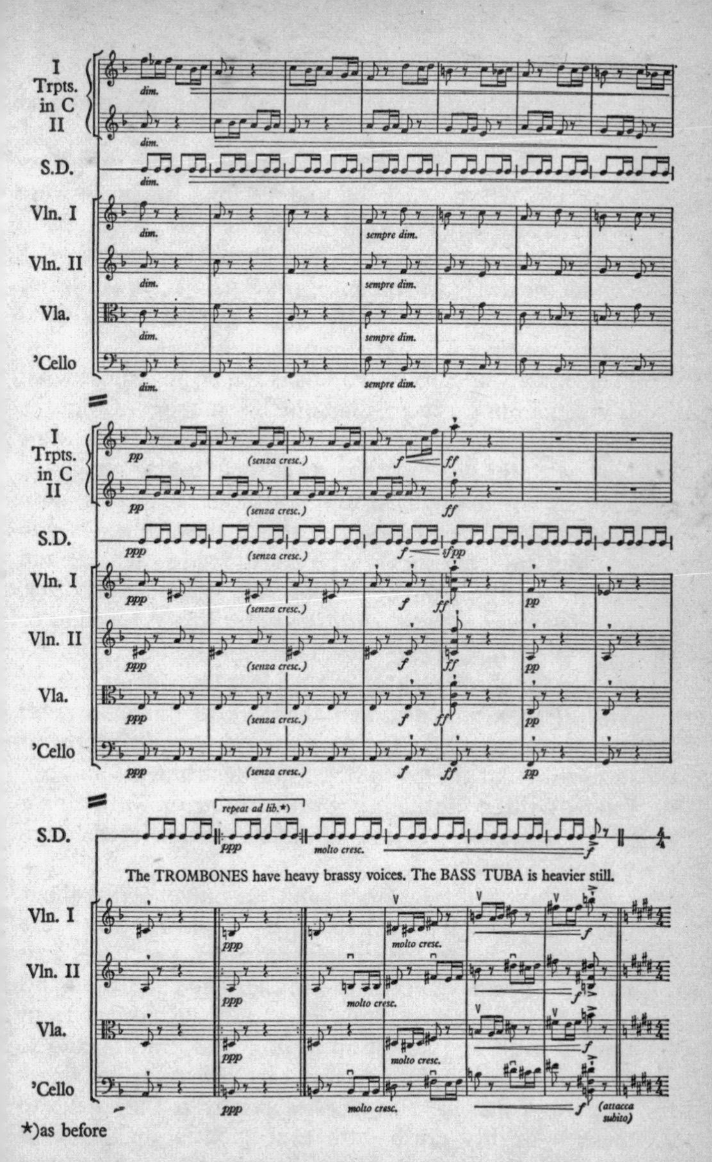

*)as before

Part of the score from Britten's The Young Person's Guide To The Orchestra

conduct Beethoven, and these had to be handed to him on a silver salver.

Conductors often start their career playing in an orchestra – Arturo Toscanini and Sir John Barbirolli were both cellists – and this kind of experience is very useful in teaching a conductor to see the players' point of view. A conductor needs to recognise the particular qualities of each instrument, to know what they do and what difficulties they will have in some pieces.

He must study every work as a whole and know what is going on in every part, and he has in front of him the full orchestral score which is always set out in the same way, with the woodwind parts at the top, then the brass, the percussion, the harp, and last of all the strings, with the double-bass down on the very bottom line. As you can see, the score shows who is playing in each bar and also how they should be playing, that is, louder or softer, faster or more slowly, with the notes joined together or hammered out separately. These instructions are expressed in words such as *crescendo, diminuendo, presto, lento, legato, staccato,* and they are in Italian because Italy was for so long first in music. If you are interested in picking out the parts of certain instruments and can follow written music, it is worth buying or borrowing a pocket score, which is a miniature version of the conductor's score.

The players, on the other hand, are only worried about their part, and if you happen to be sitting above the orchestra and can look down on them, you'll see that some players have very little music. The percussion and brass players, for example may only be needed from time to time, and not at all in some movements, and so their parts may only be a few bars. They need to know when to come in, however, especially if they have to make a mighty crash with the cymbals, and so their music also tells them how many bars they have, and it is up to them to count these and make sure they come in at the right place. Usually if they haven't been playing for some time their music will include a few bars before their entry, and the conductor will also make some sign to bring them in.

As the only person who hears all the instruments together, the conductor has to make sure that they are evenly balanced, won't drown the soloist, and are aware of his or her needs. He (and most conductors are men, though there are one or two women) will probably discuss the piece with the soloist, and if their ideas are very different, they will have to reach a compromise. Conductors are usually sympathetic to young players, and once they have made the grade they are not likely to want to play with conductors who see the music differently.

One of the best ways of understanding how interpretations of music can differ is to listen to one of those record programmes on which the speaker is comparing various performances of the same work. You'll be surprised how many different approaches there are: differences of speed, emphasis, sound quality, and above all emotional sympathy, because many performers develop a special understanding of certain composers. But the conductor shouldn't be too concerned with his own ideas. He is, as Sir Adrian Boult put it, 'the servant of the composer', and his job was summed up by the famous conductor Leopold Stokowski as 'our privilege and our necessity [is] to try and realise what was in the soul of the composer, and to make that alive again'.

Conductors help to set fashions in interpretations and to introduce new ideas and discoveries. In recent years musicians and scholars have tried to work out how early music may have sounded when it was first written, and it has been recognised that many of our ideas were based on nineteenth-century versions of great music rather than on what the composer actually wrote.

One of the most obvious changes has been in our attitude to Handel, whose music used to be performed by large orchestras and huge choirs. But this may not have been what Handel had in mind, and smaller groups such as the Academy of St Martin-in-the-Fields have helped to make popular, performances of Handel and other composers of his time that seem more authentic – though as we have only written records to go on, it's partly guesswork. Some orchestras take this re-creation of the past even further and use old instruments of the same period as the music, and if you like Bach, listen to some of the records made by Nikolaus Harnoncourt and his group of musicians called the Vienna Concentus Musicus and see if you prefer them to a modern orchestra playing Bach.

Although conductors make their reputation among fellow musicians by their knowledge and insight, the public often can't judge this and looks for other things. Some conductors are very exciting to watch, some get on with the job very quietly, others bring with them a glamour and charisma that is immediately sensed by the audience.

This was particularly the case with Sir Malcolm Sargent, who was very popular with audiences but not much admired by players. Many of them distrusted his smooth appearance, the way he was always immaculately dressed down to the carnation in his buttonhole, but Sir Malcolm felt that a concert was a special occasion, something worth dressing up for, and he wanted the audience to share this feeling. He was marvellous at inspiring huge choirs to sing their hearts out (these were the days when the *Messiah* was done on a grand scale), and he loved the kind of occasion such as the Last Night of the Proms when the audience joined in. The players may have disapproved but audiences loved him, and he left a gap that has not yet been filled.

Sir Thomas Beecham was a very different kind of conductor and a great favourite with players. He was a perfectionist, and it was said of him that he 'could make any orchestra play fifty per cent better than it knew it could – and nobody knew how he did it'. A rich man – his fortune came from the family business of Beecham's pills – he spent his money and his life in the service of music, trying to establish a proper opera company in Britain, founding his own orchestras (the London Philharmonic and the Royal Philharmonic), and championing the music of Delius and Sibelius. Many of his records have been reissued, and although the sound quality is not up to today's best, there is no mistaking the sensitivity and force of Sir Thomas's personality. He lived at a time when he could afford the luxury of individuality, could afford to set his own standards and speak his mind, and his rudeness was that of a man who put dedication to music first.

It's easy to spot the conductor, but the players too have their set places which have been worked out so that every instrument can be clearly heard. The conductor obviously needs to know where to find everyone, though some conductors do sometimes make slight changes. Sir Adrian Boult, for example, likes the second violins on his right, whereas they're usually on the left next to the first violins.

The exact number of players varies, depending on the orchestra and what they're playing, but in a major symphony orchestra such as the London Symphony there are sixteen first violins, fourteen second violins, twelve violas, ten cellos, eight double-basses, four flutes, two oboes and a cor anglais, three clarinets plus a bass clarinet, three bassoons, eight horns (most music doesn't need more than four), four trumpets, three trombones plus a bass trombone, one tuba, two timpani, three percussion, and two harps.

The seating plan shows you who sits where, but it's even more important to know what they each sound like.

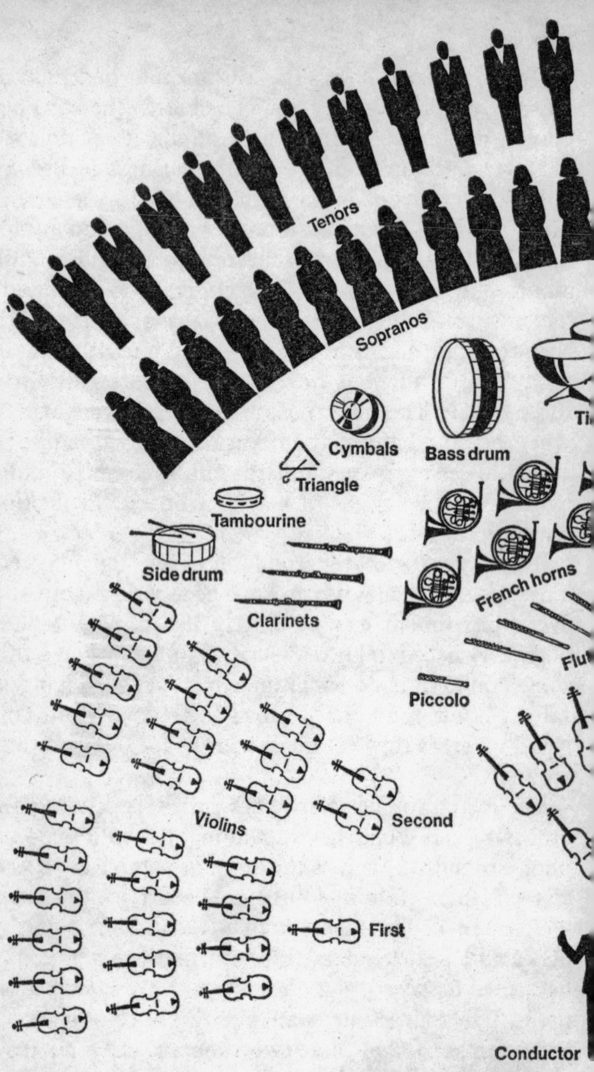

The instruments of the orchestra and a choir in their usual positions. The number of instruments shown are the maximum possible in each case

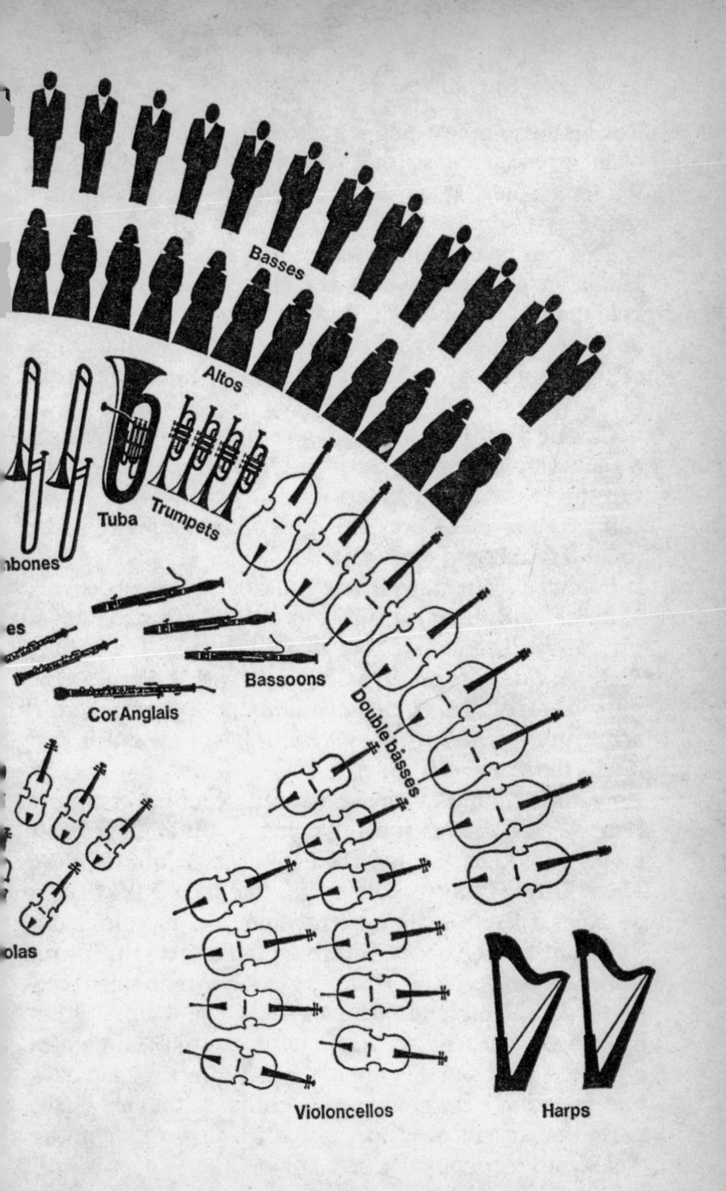
Basses
Altos
Tuba
Trumpets
Bassoons
Cor Anglais
Double basses
Violoncellos
Harps

The best way of learning is by keeping your eyes and ears open at concerts, so that you can link an instrument with the sound it makes and see how this fits into the music as a whole.

This can be difficult if you're sitting a long way back, but in many concert halls the cheapest seats are often behind or overlooking the orchestra, so that you can look down on them, see what they're up to, and get their view of the conductor – which is much more interesting than his back view.

Closing your eyes and trying to guess who's playing is a good way of getting through the boring passages that turn up in even the greatest music. And knowing what's going on can make even the most daunting music easier to understand and appreciate.

If you're at the stage where you can't tell an oboe from a clarinet and aren't sure what sort of noise the trombones make, try listening to Benjamin Britten's *The Young Person's Guide to the Orchestra*. It was written as the soundtrack of a documentary film about the orchestra, and Britten made such a marvellous job of the music that it tells the story on its own.

He took a tune by the seventeenth-century composer Henry Purcell as his starting point, and it is played first by all the orchestra and then by each section in turn. Then Britten plays about with the theme so that it becomes a lively little tune for flute and piccolo and a slow tune for the oboes. He works through all the instruments, giving each of them a variation that suits their particular talents, and then puts the whole thing together by bringing in each instrument in turn until the orchestra is back in one piece. Finally, the brass bring back Purcell's tune sounding very grand and splendid. Britten may have started off to give a lesson, but what he wrote is music that stands triumphantly on its own.

7 Musical forms

When you go to a concert, even if you don't know some of the music on the programme, you'll have some idea of what you can expect to hear from the way it's described, just as you might choose a book because it's a novel, a biography or a true story. Words like *concerto* or *symphony* don't help you decide whether you'll like the piece or not, but they may help you find your way round the music because they tell you something about its shape.

Although writing music is a magical business to most of us, and a good tune may just come out of the air, musical forms provide composers with a frame or outline within which to develop their ideas. Just as if you decide to paint a picture, the size and shape of your paper or canvas will influence the scale and compass of your painting.

Overtures, sonatas, quartets, concertos and symphonies are the sizes and shapes of music. They contain certain patterns of contrast and balance and these basic patterns, far from restricting composers, help them to sort out their ideas and often inspire them.

You may remember that when we were looking at the violin, we found that the first kind of music it played was dances. Although the dances themselves may originally have been part of primitive religious services at which people prayed for fine weather and good crops, the Christian church disapproved of dancing and it was at court and in the great houses that the old dances were gradually transformed into very civilised entertainments. When string orchestras became the fashion – and even earlier – composers began to arrange some of the dances in a more sophisticated way.

Different kinds of dances were strung together to form a *suite*, and to provide contrast, dances of different speeds and moods were chosen, so that a leisurely *allemande* might be followed by a lively *courante* which, as its name suggests, is a quick running sort of dance. Then would come a slow stately *sarabande*, and the suite would be rounded off with a *gigue* or *jig*, which was another fast lively dance. These were the basic dances, but *minuets*, *gavottes*, *bourrées* and *passepieds* were often added.

Bach wrote a number of suites along these lines and so did Handel. They are easy to enjoy, because they were intended as entertainments and it's not always easy to respond to dance rhythms which don't get off the ground unless they're lively and easy to follow. That they are also very beautiful music will be obvious if you listen to one of Bach's suites, such as the one (*No. 3 in D*) with the famous *Air on the G string*.

It wasn't only Baroque composers who wrote suites. Later ones include Bizet's *L'Arlesienne*, Grieg's *Peer Gynt*, Stravinsky's *The Firebird* and William Walton's *Façade*. Although you won't find any gavottes or gigues in them, the idea of dance is never far away – a great deal of ballet music has been arranged into suites – and the movements tend to be short and contrasting.

One very popular kind of dance that escaped from the suite was the minuet, a graceful stately dance much enjoyed at the court of the extravagant French king Louis XIV. Both Haydn and Mozart used minuets in their symphonies, and they often had a middle section that at first was played by only three players and thus known as a trio.

There was no limit to the number of dances in a suite – it could be as many as six or seven – but before long composers turned their attention to a form that involved more than just grouping dances together. At first the word *sonata* simply meant any music that was played rather than sung, and the so-called *chamber sonata* wasn't very different from a suite, though the *church sonata* kept well away from the dance. But the sonata soon developed a shape of its own, and this shape was to have a profound effect on chamber music, concertos, and symphonies. Today a sonata is a work for one or two players, and there are sonatas for all sorts of instruments from the flute to the trombone.

It started as a simple single movement such as you can hear in the sonatas of Scarlatti, but C. P. Bach (one of the great Bach's many sons), Haydn and Mozart expanded it to three movements, the first of which was quick and forceful, the second slow and lyrical, and the third some kind of dance. Beethoven added a fourth movement to some of his sonatas, and his magnificent thirty-two piano sonatas show what variety was possible within the form. He was not content to write sonatas that were simply charming and light-hearted – though some have these qualities – but he also made the sonata profoundly serious and tragic.

As well as being a piece of music in three or four movements, the word sonata also refers in particular to the pattern of the first movement, which has a very definite design. There are three distinct parts, called the exposition, the development, and the recapitulation, and in order to understand what goes on in each part, you must think of the movement as a kind of musical drama. This comparison is used by Antony Hopkins in his book *Talk-*

ing About Sonatas, and I have borrowed it from him because I couldn't think of a better way of explaining sonata form.

In the exposition we meet the group of characters the play is to be about, and gradually we begin to recognise one person as the chief character. Musically, he is a tune that revolves round a particular note called the *tonic,* which is the most important note of the key in which the movement is written. After the first tune has been introduced, we get the feeling that someone else is expected, and after the music has prepared us for the new arrival, in she comes and changes the whole mood. Her relationship to the first character we met is established by a precise musical link: her tune probably centres round a note called the *dominant,* which is the fifth note of the key and second in importance only to the tonic.

Now that we have met both the main characters, the plot begins to develop. We learn a lot more about both of them, much of it unexpected and perhaps surprising, so that the tunes of the first part seem to be wearing different disguises. The final recapitulation takes us back to the opening, but by now we know the main characters or tunes fairly well, and when they turn up again we see them in a new light.

This is a very simple account of the basic pattern of sonata form, and you may be disappointed and puzzled if the next time you listen to a sonata it doesn't seem to follow any of these signposts. Don't worry. The most important reaction to any piece of music is what it says to you. The message may be sad or happy, lighthearted or serious, or the piece may take your fancy because you like a certain sequence of notes without knowing why. The message is unlikely to be about whether or not the music follows the sonata pattern and if not, why not, but you may be aware of surprises and dramatic contrasts, and this is why sonata form is important to composers.

Just as a playwright finds it helpful to organise his play into three acts and recognises that it is good theatre to end a scene with an intriguing line or a climax, so a composer may find the sonata form helps him to present his musical ideas as effectively as possible. And if you're really curious and want to find out a composer's secrets and what goes on behind the scenes, you'll need to know a lot more about the theoretical side of music. But if you haven't the time or the opportunity to take these things further, it doesn't mean that you will enjoy music any the less.

If you like a particular instrument, the sonatas written for it will give you a good idea of all the different things it can say. And there are plenty of sonatas to choose from, especially for the piano or violin. Haydn wrote about sixty piano sonatas, Mozart twenty, and Beethoven thirty-two. Beethoven explored the sonata so thoroughly that he didn't leave much for the composers who came after him to do. Schubert, Chopin, Schumann and Brahms all wrote piano sonatas, but they also turned to other forms with a different kind of structure.

Although Scarlatti's sonatas are charming and Haydn's are concerned with grace and symmetry, Mozart and especially Beethoven used the sonata to express passionate, rebellious, tragic ideas. Beethoven's best-known piano sonata is probably the *Moonlight*, but he was concerned with far more than painting a pretty picture. His piano sonatas are a record of the spiritual journey he made from the enthusiasm of youth to a time when he was cut off from the world by deafness and wrote music that he could only hear in his imagination. They are a bridge between the classical world of Haydn and Mozart and a new Romantic world of personal feelings.

Sonata form was also very important to the *symphony*, which is in a sense a sonata for the whole orchestra. Symphonies began as music that was played before an opera – a kind of overture – but composers soon found that audiences went on talking and didn't pay much attention, and so they transferred their symphonies to the concert-hall.

The first ones had only one movement, usually divided into contrasting quick and slow tunes, and the delightful short symphonies of William Boyce – all eight of which fit on to one record – are a good example of such pieces. But the symphony soon spread out into three or four movements, and these followed the general plan of a long first movement marked *adagio* (in a leisurely manner) or *allegro* (fast and lively), a slow second movement, then a minuet, and finally a conclusion that was often very fast (*presto*) or in the form of a *rondo*, in which the same tune keeps coming back after a contrasting tune to form an A B A C A pattern.

Although he didn't invent the symphony, Haydn has been called the 'Father of the Symphony' because he wrote so many (over a hundred) and made the form popular. At one time only a few of his symphonies were still played, but Decca had the courage to start recording them all in splendid performances conducted by Antal Dorati, and the project has been a great success and shown what a marvellous composer Haydn was. All the symphonies are a delight, but if you want to start with an obvious winner try *No. 101 in D*, the *Clock* symphony, so called because the slow movement opens with a ticking rhythm.

Mozart would probably have made an even greater contribution to the symphony if he had lived longer (he died aged thirty-five). As it is, his three greatest symphonies, Nos 39, 40 and 41 (nicknamed the *Jupiter*) were all written in the incredible space of six weeks. The ideas and themes in them flow with a mastery and inventiveness possible only to genius.

But the world in which Mozart lived was changing

rapidly, and the storm clouds of revolution – the French Revolution began in 1789 – were to be mirrored in the symphonies that Beethoven started writing in 1799. He found the minuet too tame, and put in its place the lively *scherzo*, which is not always a joke (though that is the literal meaning of the word) but often has a rather grim sense of humour.

Beethoven made the symphony much longer – his *Third* lasts fifty minutes, his *Ninth* seventy minutes – and he introduced a more personal meaning into the *Eroica* symphony, which was originally dedicated to Napoleon, whom Beethoven greatly admired until he got too big for his boots and began to call himself Emperor. His own heroic approach to life is well expressed by the *Fifth* symphony, which begins with the famous three short notes and a long one which Beethoven described as Fate knocking at the door.

The Sixth, *Pastoral*, symphony is a wonderful piece of descriptive writing with such effects as the sound of the nightingale, the cuckoo, a thunderstorm, and the beautiful shepherd's song of thanksgiving after the storm. The *Seventh* has a noble very impressive slow movement, the *Eighth* is Beethoven in a cheerful mood, and then his titanic energy burst forth in the *Ninth* in a great shout of choral exultation. The orchestra was no longer powerful enough, he needed the human voice too to join in the final 'Ode to Joy' which celebrates the brotherhood of man and his worship of a loving god beyond the stars.

By this stage Beethoven's deafness was such that he was unable to hear even the might of his last symphony, and one of the greatest tunes in the world was written in sad, one might think overwhelming, conditions. A visitor found Beethoven composing 'in the most appalling disorder – music, money, clothing on the floor, the bed unmade, broken coffee-cups upon the table, the open pianoforte with scarcely any string left and thickly covered with dust, while he himself was wrapped in a shabby old dressing-gown.'

Beethoven had set the symphony free, and his successors continued the Romantic tradition in which the artist concentrated on his own experience and what made it unique.

Schubert expressed tender poetical feelings in his music, and his symphonies are rich in enchanting melodies. The best-known are the last two. The *Unfinished* symphony got its name from the fact that it has only two movements. It is not known whether Schubert meant to finish it or just forgot about it – he wrote so easily that he didn't take great care of his compositions – but it isn't now thought that it was finished and lost. The *Great C major* symphony – called *Great* because it is so long and to distinguish it from his other symphony in the same key – is a powerful work that is full of feeling. Sadly it was never played during Schubert's lifetime because orchestras found it too difficult.

The next great innovator, Berlioz, was inspired by literary ideas and wrote symphonies about Romeo and Juliet and Byron's poem *Childe Harold*. His extrordinary *Symphonie fantastique* had the sub-title 'Episodes in the life of an artist' and reflected an unhappy love affair. But although Berlioz started from non-musical ideas, he wrote genuine symphonies that reflect a dramatic, highly original approach.

If he took the symphony far away from the old classical ideas, Brahms looked back to Beethoven and wrote powerful uplifting works, the result of careful craftsmanship. Tchaikovsky, on the other hand, lacked a sense of form but brought to the symphony the dramatic intensity and excitement that made his ballet music so successful. His last and greatest symphony, the *Pathetique*, is very emotional, and the second movement contains one of his most famous tunes.

A good tune is a useful lifeline when you're starting to listen to symphonies, and one of the easiest to remember turns up in Dvorak's *New World* symphony, written when the Czech composer was working in America. He visited some of his fellow-countrymen who had settled there and heard some of the Negro folk-music, though the beautiful tune 'Going Home' is not a real Negro melody.

There isn't the space to mention all the other composers who wrote symphonies, except for someone who became very popular in the 1960s. For Mahler, the symphony had to embrace the world, and he wrote on a grand scale. His *Eighth* symphony earned the nickname *Symphony of a Thousand* because of the vast number of players needed. When it was performed in Liverpool Cathedral in 1965, there were 180 instrumentalists and 520 singers.

British composers weren't equal to the challenge of the symphony until this century. Those you are most likely to hear are the two noble symphonies by Elgar and the works of Vaughan Williams, such as the descriptive *London Symphony* and his *Sinfonia Antarctica*, originally written for a film about the great explorer Scott of the Antarctic.

The other great orchestral form that developed alongside the symphony was the *concerto*, which began with a small group of players pitted against the rest of the orchestra. Such *concerti grossi* (or grand concertos) were fashionable in the seventeenth and early eighteenth centuries, and much of this splendid spirited music had been rediscovered and popularised by small chamber orchestras such as the Academy of St Martin-in-the-Fields. You can sample it at its best in the twelve elegant, assured concertos (Op. 6) by Handel, which positively dance along.

The arrival of public concerts and star performers encouraged the development of concertos for just one soloist. They were usually in three movements, the first based on sonata form, the second a slow movement, and the third often a lively rondo, and there was also a *cadenza*, a solo passage devised by the soloist to dazzle the audience by his virtuosity. The cadenzas seem to have got rather out of hand so that they disrupted the work as a whole, and after a while composers began to write their own. Beethoven wrote cadenzas for his first four piano concertos, but omitted one from the *Emperor* because the whole concerto was a big enough showpiece for any pianist.

The best-known concertos have already been mentioned under the appropriate instruments, but if you don't already have a favourite, make a start with Beethoven's piano concertos or the famous romantic piano concertos by Schumann, Grieg, Tchaikovsky, and Rachmaninov. They are all works that you will hear many times – perhaps too often – and they make their greatest impact at the beginning of one's musical experience when everything's new and one's responses are still fresh.

If concertos are easy listening, chamber music isn't. It has been described as 'the music of friends' and it probably gives its greatest reward to the players. As its name suggests, it is music suitable for a small room, a room where friends meet to make music, and its most popular form, the *string quartet*, calls for two violins, a viola, and a cello.

Once again the form owes much to Haydn – he's also been called the 'Father of the String Quartet' – but although he did much to develop it, its roots go back to the small groups, or consorts as they were called, of the sixteenth and seventeenth centuries. You will probably get the chance to hear some of this early *ensemble* music, because it is being revived as more people become interested in old instruments.

Chamber music isn't only string quartets; it also includes *trios, quintets, sextets* and *octets,* and the piano and various wind instruments sometimes take part. The music is mostly in sonata form, and it is a great test of a composer's skill because with so few instruments every note is important and there is no mass of sound to cover up poor writing.

As you might expect, the great quartet composers are Haydn, Mozart, and Beethoven, all of whom wrote masterpieces in this form. You may find them difficult to grasp at first, and you probably need to be a musician to appreciate the finer points. The supreme achievement is said to be the last quartets of Beethoven, and those who have mastered their complexity speak of a musical experience that seems to be on a higher plane.

8 Music for singing

Although once they arrived on the scene the instruments of the orchestra soon took over music, for hundreds of years a much older instrument, the human voice, had reigned supreme.

Pope Gregory I, who was to give his name to a type of singing called *Gregorian chant*, lived in the sixth century AD, and the tunes that he gathered together had already existed for centuries. He sorted them out, got rid of those he thought unsuitable, and produced a collection of hymns and settings of the mass and the other services that were to be used throughout the Church – and are still used today.

The services were sung by monks, usually without any accompaniment, and they were sometimes divided into two groups so that one answered the other. In time the simple *plainsong* with its one-line melody began to develop other parts, first a lower line for those who just naturally sang lower, and then a top line or *descant*, and before long all the parts were no longer singing the same tune but exploring much more interesting possibilities.

But the Church didn't have the monopoly of vocal music. There was also a strong tradition of popular songs handed down from one generation to the next, there were professional singers called *minstrels*, whose job it was to entertain their masters, and the masters themselves also began to try their hand at singing, often making up songs that spoke of their longing for some unattainable love. And such songs, which began in France, gradually spread to the rest of Europe.

The idea of *madrigals* came originally from Italy, where composers such as Orlando di Lasso, Palestrina, and later Claudio Monteverdi, used the skill they had developed in church music to set words that had nothing to do with religion.

Madrigals celebrated instead the joys and sorrows of love, the beauty of nature, the pleasures of springtime, and the titles of some of the best-known English ones – 'All creatures now are merry-minded', 'The sweet and merry month', 'Now is the month of Maying', 'The silver swan', 'Sorrow consumes me,' 'Retire, my troubled soul' – – give a good idea of some of the favourite subjects and moods.

After various collections of Italian madrigals had appeared in England, the idea caught on and singing madrigals became a popular accomplishment in the best circles. They were *part-songs*, sometimes with as many as six different parts woven together, and they were usually unaccompanied, though the viols did sometimes join in.

Madrigals attracted the talents of most of the leading Elizabethan composers, and in 1601 a famous collection of them called *The Triumphs of Oriana* was published. It was put together by Thomas Morley (famous for his song 'It was a lover and his lass') and was planned as a tribute to Queen Elizabeth, the Oriana of the title. Each song ended with the words, 'Long live fair Oriana', and among the twenty-three composers eager to pay homage to their queen were Thomas Tomkins, Thomas Weelkes, and John Wilbye.

Madrigals are still popular with small groups of expert singers, and their charms include some beautiful poetry and ravishing music. They do demand a gift for sight-reading, but if you're not up to singing them, they are also enchanting to listen to.

As in Italy, the composers of madrigals also wrote church music, and many of them were members of the king's own band of musicians known as the Chapel Royal. It was founded at the beginning of the twelfth century, and its members travelled round with the court and performed the daily services wherever the king was staying. The musicians were called the Gentlemen of the Chapel Royal, and there were also choirboys who were chosen from all over the country and educated in a special choir school. Today the choir still performs at the chapel in St James's Palace, and the boys still wear the scarlet and gold uniform that dates from Tudor times.

The Chapel Royal reached great musical heights during the reign of Queen Elizabeth I, when the gentlemen included such fine musicians and composers as Thomas Tallis, William Byrd and, later, Orlando Gibbons and Thomas Tomkins. Under the Tudors the Church passed through the crisis that resulted in Henry VIII setting himself up as head of the Church of England, and the passing of the old religion brought a gradual changeover to services in English instead of Latin. English church music also separated itself from the Roman tradition, and Byrd, although he remained a Roman Catholic, gave the new church some of its finest music.

In those days choirs trained to sing the services every day existed in churches, chapels and cathedrals all over the kingdom, and there are still some choir schools left where boys are given the unique training that makes it possible for them to master vast amounts of music from Byrd to the present day. It means living away from home, daily practices, having to stay on at Christmas and Easter, but the boys seem to thrive on hard work and are very sad when their voices break, which often happens when they are around the age of thirteen.

One of the most famous such choirs is that of King's College, Cambridge, which is made up of sixteen boy *trebles* and fourteen undergraduates, who sing the *alto*, *tenor* and *bass* parts. It is known all over the world through its records and broadcasts of the Festival of Nine Lessons and Carols which is always held on Christmas Eve. There is no mistaking the purity of their sound, which may owe something to the acoustics of the magnificent sixteenth-century chapel. Other fine choirs are those of St John's, Cambridge, Magdalen College and Christ Church Cathedral, Oxford, St Paul's and Westminster Abbey.

The mass is the most important service of the Roman Catholic Church, and there have been many settings of it, usually of the Kyrie, Gloria, Credo, Sanctus and Agnus Dei sections. Early masterpieces were written by Orlando di Lasso and Palestrina, who took his name from the small town near Rome where he was born. He spent his life in the service of the Church, first as a choirboy and then as a choirmaster, and he was described on his coffin as 'Prince of Music'. His music is very pure, as though written by an angel rather than a man, and it conveys the sense of mystery that lies at the heart of the mass.

It also became the fashion to set only parts of the mass, such as the Kyrie or the Gloria, and Vivaldi's *Gloria* recently proved very popular when it was performed at the Proms. It's lively music – the *Domine Fili Unigenite* is positively jaunty – that would surely convert anyone who thinks religious music has to be sober and dull.

Bach's splendid *Mass in B minor* started out as only two movements – written to try and please the Duke of Saxony – and the rest were added later. It is an impressive work: some of the choruses are in six or eight parts so

TIME CHART OF COMPOSERS

1550 1600 1650 1700 1750 1800 1850 1900 1950 1980

PALESTRINA (*c.* 1525–1594)
BYRD (1543–1623)
DOWLAND (1563–1626)
MONTEVERDI (1567–1643)
LULLY (1632–1687)
CORELLI (1653–1713)
PURCELL (1658–1695)
COUPERIN (1668–1733)
VIVALDI (1678–1741)
BACH (1685–1750)
SCARLATTI (1685–1757)
HANDEL (1685–1759)
HAYDN (1732–1809)
MOZART (1756–1791)
BEETHOVEN (1770–1827)
ROSSINI (1792–1868)
SCHUBERT (1797–1828)
DONIZETTI (1797–1848)
BERLIOZ (1803–1869)
MENDELSSOHN (1809–1847)
CHOPIN (1810–1849)
SCHUMANN (1810–1856)
LISZT (1811–1886)

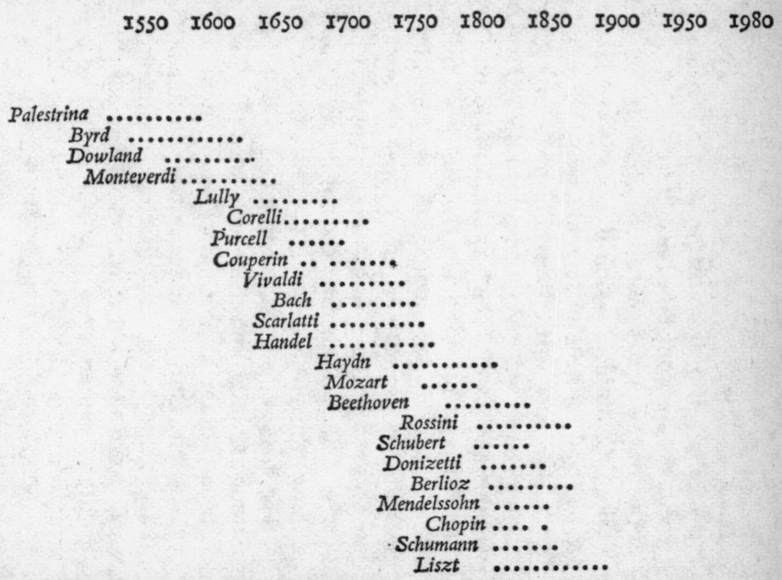

Palestrina ....
Byrd ....
Dowland ....
Monteverdi ....
Lully ....
Corelli ....
Purcell ......
Couperin .. ..
Vivaldi ....
Bach ....
Scarlatti ....
Handel ....
Haydn ....
Mozart ......
Beethoven ....
Rossini ....
Schubert ......
Donizetti ....
Berlioz ....
Mendelssohn ......
Chopin .... .
Schumann ....
Liszt ....

WAGNER (1813–1883)	
VERDI (1813–1901)	*Verdi*
OFFENBACH (1819–1880)	*Offenback*
JOHANN STRAUSS (1825–1899)	*Johann Strauss*
BRAHMS (1833–1897)	*Brahms*
SAINT-SAËNS (1835–1921)	*Saint-Saëns*
BIZET (1838–1875)	*Bizet*
TCHAIKOVSKY (1840–1893)	*Tchaikovsky*
DVOŘÁK (1841–1904)	*Dvořák*
SULLIVAN (1842–1900)	*Sullivan*
GRIEG (1843–1907)	*Grieg*
FAURÉ (1845–1924)	*Fauré*
ELGAR (1857–1934)	*Elgar*
PUCCINI (1858–1924)	*Puccini*
WOLF (1860–1903)	*Wolf*
MAHLER (1860–1911)	*Mahler*
DEBUSSY (1862–1918)	*Debussy*
R. STRAUSS (1864–1949)	*R. Strauss*
VAUGHAN WILLIAMS (1872–1958)	*Vaughan Williams*
RACHMANINOV (1873–1943)	*Rachmaninov*
SCHOENBERG (1874–1951)	*Schoenberg*
BARTÓK (1881–1945)	*Bartók*
STRAVINSKY (1882–1971)	*Stravinsky*
WEBERN (1883–1945)	*Webern*
PROKOFIEV (1891–1953)	*Prokofiev*
GERSHWIN (1898–1937)	*Gershwin*
RODGERS (1902–	*Rodgers'*
SHOSTAKOVITCH (1906–1975)	*Shostakovitch*
WALTON (1902–	*Walton*
BRITTEN (1913–1976)	*Britten*
STOCKHAUSEN (1928–	*Stockhausen*

that they build up massive slabs of sound, and the news of the resurrection is announced in a thrilling way.

Haydn was called on to write a number of masses for the Esterhazy family, and at the end of his life he was invited to return to the princely household – which had earlier dismissed the band – in order to write a mass once a year to celebrate the name-day of the prince's wife. Haydn welcomed the security offered him in old age, and the six masses of his last years are among his greatest achievements. They are choral symphonies to the glory of God, but the first, *Missa in tempore belli* (*Mass in time of war*) also reflected Austria's current war against the French in the important part played by drums and trumpets. And the greatest of the masses was the one written to celebrate a victory by Nelson, and known since as the *Nelson* mass.

Mozart too wrote masses, and his last one was the result of a strange and tragic joke. He was visited by a mysterious stranger dressed all in grey who asked Mozart to write a requiem mass (a mass praying for the rest of the soul of the departed) for an unknown patron. Mozart, who was very depressed and in a poor state of health, came to believe that his visitor had been death itself, and that he was writing his own requiem. He didn't live to finish it – but it turned out afterwards that the request had come from a rather eccentric nobleman who had commissioned the mass in honour of his late wife.

Beethoven wrote a mighty mass, the *Missa Solemnis*, and so did Berlioz, whose *Grande Masse des Morts* isn't often performed because it needs such huge forces. Berlioz was asked to write it by the French government, and in his *Memoirs* he gives a very funny account of the first performance, which only took place after a lot of bureaucratic wrangling. Berlioz was persuaded to let the official conductor on state occasions take charge, but took the precaution of staying just behind him. At the crucial moment when four bands herald the Last Judgement, the conductor calmly laid down his baton and produced his snuff-box, and disaster was only averted because Berlioz leapt on to the rostrum and took charge.

Other nineteenth-century composers who wrote requiem masses were Verdi, whose work has the drama you'd expect from an opera composer, and Fauré, whose mass is a simple expression of faith.

The continuing importance of the mass was shown by the popularity of Benjamin Britten's *War Requiem*, written in 1961 for the opening of the new cathedral at Coventry. It uses the traditional Latin text and the poems of Wilfred Owen, a young poet who was killed in the First World War, and on the title page Britten quoted Owen's description of his poems: 'My subject is war, and the pity of war. The Poetry is in the pity . . . All a poet can do today is warn'. It is a message that explains why the work was an immediate success.

Nowadays many of these masses are more often performed in concert-halls than in churches, but an even more popular form of religious music, the *oratorio*, has spent most of its life outside church.

It began around 1600 at the Oratory (hence oratorio) of St Philip Neri in Rome, where dramatic settings of religious texts were staged as a kind of sacred opera. The idea soon spread to Germany, and there it was developed by Heinrich Schutz, who wrote three versions of the passion story.

The two most famous composers of the Baroque period, Bach and Handel, both wrote oratorios, but their approach was very different. Bach wrote as a devout Christian who spent much of his time in the organ-loft, Handel as a man of the world who spent much of his time in the theatre.

Bach's duties as choirmaster at Weimar involved composing a *cantata* each month to celebrate the most important days in the church calendar. They were 'musical sermons', and Bach often made use of *chorales* (traditional hymn-tunes) that were familiar to the congregation, who could then join in the final chorus. More than two hundred of these cantatas have survived – each a small masterpiece of vocal music – and they are gradually all being recorded in authentic and superb performances by the Vienna Concentus Musicus under the direction of Nikolaus Harnoncourt.

In some ways they are easier to listen to than the great and better-known *St John* and *St Matthew Passions*, in which the soloists reflect on the meaning of the familiar story of the death of Christ.

Handel's approach was more dramatic, and although he was to make the oratorio the supreme expression of English religious emotion, he began writing oratorios by chance. An admirer put on a private performance of one of his earlier works as a tribute, and Handel was so pleased that he decided to stage it in public. It had been performed by the children of the Chapel Royal, but the idea of putting on a Bible story in a theatre caused an uproar, and the Bishop of London sternly forbade any such thing.

But Handel was not easily defeated. He revised the work, turned it into a musical drama staged without costumes, scenery or action, and *Esther* was such a success that it was patronised by the Royal family. It was to be followed in time by other such dramas – *Saul, Israel in Egypt, Samson, Judas Maccabaeus* and, most famous of all, *Messiah*.

Handel started composing *Messiah* on 22nd August 1741, and finished it less than a month later. It was written when his fortunes were at one of their lowest points, and the speed with which he wrote suggests that he was truly inspired. His servant found him in tears after he had written the Hallelujah Chorus, and Handel told him, 'I did think I did see all Heaven before me, and the great God himself'.

Messiah was first performed in Dublin on 13th April 1742, and it was an immediate success. At a later performance the King himself is said to have been so moved that he leapt to his feet – and as the court had to rise too, this may be the origin of the custom that the audience always stands for the Hallelujah Chorus. It is typical of Handel and his times that he was not against using a good tune more than once – there were no records to make some music too familiar – and the Hallelujah Chorus turns up again as the finale to the *Anthem for the Foundling Hospital*, a charity to which Handel was very attached.

Haydn, inspired perhaps by Handel's example, made chorus as fine as 'The heavens are telling' in *The Creation*, which tells how God made the world and starts with a musical description of chaos and a whispered chorus that bursts into life at the word 'light' at the end of the phrase 'and there was light'. *The Seasons*, though it lacks a chorus as fine as 'The heavens are telling', in *The Creation* describes the sights and sounds of the countryside with charming freshness.

In Victorian England vast amateur choirs became popular and oratorios were the order of the day. They were performed at the Three Choirs Festival, held in turn in the cathedral cities of Gloucester, Hereford and Worcester, and the Birmingham Festival took the lead in commissioning new works. Mendelssohn pleased choirs and audiences with *Elijah* which has some exciting choruses calling on the false god Baal and a dramatic chorus in which the Lord, after failing to turn up in the tempest, the earthquake or the fire, appears as a small still voice.

He himself conducted the first performance, and had a happier experience of English choral singing than a later composer, Edward Elgar. The Festival had commissioned his *Dream of Gerontius*, which is based on a poem by Cardinal Newman that describes the journey of the soul to the next world.

The soul has to pass by a fearful pack of demons waiting to drag it down to hell, and the choir, who did not have long enough to learn this difficult music, ruined it. Elgar knew that he had written a great work – he wrote at the end of the score, 'This is the best of me . . . this, if anything of mine, is worth your memory' – and he was bitterly disappointed by the disastrous first performance. Later, he was to write two more oratorios about the life and work of the apostles, and although they are not as well-known as *Gerontius*, they are full of wonderful music.

Although the Victorians enjoyed singing on a grand scale, they also liked to sing in their own drawing-rooms and sentimental ballads and love songs were very popular.

They were a far cry from the traditional folk-songs that had survived among country people for hundreds of years, but were slowly dying out. Luckily their importance was recognised before they disappeared completely, and at the end of the nineteenth century the Folk Song Society was founded and people like Cecil Sharp and Ralph Vaughan Williams began to collect and study them. Vaughan Williams also wrote songs himself, and you may have sung the beautiful 'Linden Lea', or heard his *Songs of Travel* and *On Wenlock Edge*, six settings of poems by A. E. Housman, whose poetry also inspired another composer, George Butterworth.

The best-known recent composer of songs is Benjamin Britten, who wrote some superb songs for his friend the tenor Peter Pears including the *Seven Sonnets of Michelangelo*, the magical *Serenade* for tenor, horn and strings, and *Winter Words*, which shows Britten's marvellous response to Thomas Hardy's poetry. Many of the songs were recorded by Pears with Britten as a very sympathetic accompanist.

But for all the charm of English songs the greatest songs were written in the nineteenth century by two German composers, Franz Schubert and Hugo Wolf. They are often referred to as *Lieder*, a term used for German songs with a piano accompaniment.

Schubert wrote nearly six hundred songs expressing all sorts of moods, and he had the gift of being able to set anything to music and composing so easily that he once wrote eight songs in a day. Words sparked off his musical imagination, and he often set the scene in enchanting accompaniments. Some of his most famous songs are part of the two song-cycles *Die schöne Müllerin* and *Winterreise,* which have been beautifully interpreted by the German baritone Dietrich Fischer-Dieskau. He often sang with Gerald Moore, who turned the background job of accompanying into a star role.

The other great composer of Lieder, Hugo Wolf, also wrote wonderful piano parts, and in his songs the voice and the piano are equal partners.

Unless you understand German, it is easy to feel shut out of the meaning of Schubert's and Wolf's songs, but translations are usually available at recitals and on record sleeves, and it's worth trying to respond to the beauty of the language itself. After all, songs do give words a new shine.

9 Opera

It is hard to believe that anyone who loves music could fail to respond to the intoxicating excitement of opera, but a surprising number of music-lovers miss out on opera because they find the whole idea ridiculous.

They are put off by the absurdity of people singing about events and feelings that would at least seem more natural and convincing if they were expressed in spoken words, and in a language one could understand. They also complain that many opera stories are highly improbable and about characters who would be better off locked up somewhere safe instead of carrying on in a way that is unbelievably remote from real life. How, say the critics of opera, can one be interested in people who behave like this?

But more and more people are becoming interested, and are prepared to spend a great deal of money on what often becomes a passion. Opera is a costly form of entertainment, and in spite of huge grants from industry and public patrons such as the Arts Council, it will never be profitable. If you want to go to the opera, and especially if you want to go to any of the great opera houses of the world – Covent Garden in London, La Scala in Milan, the Metropolitan in New York, the opera house in Sydney – you can expect to pay a lot for the privilege.

And privilege is the right word, because opera began in the privileged world of courts, princes and noblemen, where it was often staged to celebrate a special occasion such as a marriage between the heirs of two great houses.

The earliest opera still performed is Monteverdi's Orfeo, which was produced at the court of Mantua in 1607. Monteverdi had begun as a very junior musician in the Duke of Gonzaga's household, and had heard of the experiments being made by a group of poets and musicians in Florence, who recited stories taken from Greek mythology to music.

These first operas had stressed the importance of the words, but Monteverdi cared more about the music. He chose a story that emphasised the power of music – Orpheus was a musician whose playing so charmed the king of the underworld that he agreed to let Orpheus's dead wife return to him – and shifted the interest from the text (known in opera as the *libretto*) to the music and invented the story-telling device known as *recitative*.

Most of the story was told in a kind of speech-like singing, and to make sure that the audience could hear the words clearly, the singer was only accompanied by a gentle instrument such as a lute or a harpsichord, which often just played simple chords that punctuated the sense of the words. In time, when the strings had learned to play softly, the recitative had a full orchestral backing, but its importance shrank as composers discovered better ways of telling the story and as audiences began to demand more songs to break up the monotony.

The French king Louis XIV was not slow to realise the marvellous possibilities of opera. He wanted operas that would contribute to his own greater glory, and these were skilfully provided by his pet composer, Jean-Baptiste Lully. He developed the role of the chorus and introduced spectacular ballets to please Louis, who loved dancing, and although he used the familiar stories of classical mythology, he presented them in a way that made audiences feel they were still important and had something new to say to them.

But audiences weren't satisfied with beautiful music. They also wanted the gods and goddesses to pop down out of the heavens trailing real clouds of glory. Such effects were costly, and destructive to the real purpose of opera, but they did establish it as exciting to look at, and theatrical illusions remained important, especially to Wagner, whose operas are full of magical effects.

London was introduced to the charms of Italian opera by Handel, who was offered the chance to write an opera as soon as he arrived. He composed *Rinaldo* in a fortnight – and became famous overnight.

He followed up his success with a string of operas that were tossed off to suit the singers who began to flock to London, and he bounced back triumphantly from the failures that were caused by jealousy of his talent and by the intrigues of rival managers. His plots were usually complicated and told in recitative broken up by songs in which a character gave a dazzling display of his or her feelings and then left the stage. Sometimes two characters sang a duet and occasionally there were a few lines for the chorus, but the solo songs (called *arias*) were all important and any composer who failed to write arias that showed off the wonderful talent of the leading singers was soon in trouble.

Handel wrote some of his finest arias for the special singers known as *castrati*. One of the most famous was Senesino, who started life as a street urchin in Siena and had such a sweet mezzo-soprano voice that it brought him fame and a fortune. It was an unnatural voice for a man, and was the result of an operation which prevented the onset of puberty and the consequent breaking of a boy's voice, but audiences didn't mind and swooned at the sound.

One of Handel's most enchanting operas, *Alcina*, has a beautiful song 'Verdi prati' that was written for the *castrato* Carestini, who was so conceited that at first he complained that the song wasn't good enough for him. It is now the most famous aria in *Alcina*, but today it is usually sung by a woman dressed up as a man. Such parts are also sung by counter-tenors such as James Bowman, whose natural voice is bass but who can produce an artificially high voice, a kind of *falsetto*. Some people find male sopranos and altos unpleasant, but they make a very distinctive sound that can be beautiful.

Handel's operas were largely forgotten until the 1920s – except for the odd song such as 'Where 'ere you walk' and 'Ombra mai fu' (better known as 'Handel's Largo') – but they are now performed regularly by the Handel Opera Society, and Joan Sutherland scored one of her biggest successes as the wicked enchantress Alcina.

But for all their charms audiences began to tire of the excessively ornamental music and improbable plots of Handel and his contemporaries, and the German composer Gluck reformed opera by stressing that music had to serve the dramatic needs of the plot instead of just decorating it. Another development was a new kind of opera, known as *opera buffa*, that didn't take itself too seriously. Its plots revolved round comic servants, amorous old men, girls who were after their money, and parted young lovers, and they were meant to make people laugh. When a company from Naples (where opera buffa had started) visited Paris, the French were delighted by their warmth and good humour, and *comic operas* soon became very popular.

Although three of Mozart's greatest operas – *The Marriage of Figaro*, *Don Giovanni* and *Cosi fan tutte* – are comedies, they are not part of the comic opera tradition because their aim and the quality of their music is far higher and more serious. As well as entertaining his audiences, Mozart also wanted to make them think about the relationships between master and servant, husband and wife, lovers, and in his *ensembles* he developed one of the highlights of opera, the way in which a group of characters can all express their separate feelings at the same time. This is impossible in a play, but some of the most exciting moments in opera come when several characters, often at cross-purposes with each other, combine in a trio, a quartet or even a sextet that weaves the strands of their various points of view into a musical whole. Here music really triumphs over words and gives us a more truthful impression of what everyone is feeling.

Mozart's last opera, *The Magic Flute*, is a masterpiece that stands out on its own. At one level it was meant to be a pantomime with songs, but no pantomime has ever had such sublime arias. Much of the dialogue is spoken not sung, and until late in the nineteenth century any opera with speech in it was thought of as a comic opera, even if it had a tragic plot. This is why Gounod's *Faust* and Bizet's *Carmen* were both classed as comic operas, though they were nothing to laugh at.

The Revolutionary atmosphere at the end of the eighteenth century transformed opera audiences, and they began to want operas that took place in their own time and dealt with spectacular dramatic events. Operas about heroes and heroines who were imprisoned and had to be rescued were very popular, and Beethoven wrote a famous example in *Fidelio*. But of course being Beethoven he went far beyond the bounds of the melodramatic plot and made it into a great call for right and freedom.

In Italy there was such a demand for new operas that composers had to work with lightning speed. Audiences liked rousing showy music that gave the singers plenty of chance to show off, and both Rossini and Donizetti were very good at pleasing them. Only a handful of their many operas are still performed today, but they include Rossini's *The Barber of Seville* with its well-known 'Figaro' song, Donizetti's *Don Pasquale*, a favourite of the great Welsh bass Geraint Evans, and his *Lucia di Lammermoor*, which has a marvellous part for the heroine that ends with her going mad. Another Italian composer who wrote thrilling arias for his leading ladies was Bellini, and in recent years Maria Callas and Joan Sutherland both enjoyed dazzling their public with the vocal gymnastics of *La Somnambula* and *Norma*.

Italy's greatest operatic composer, Giuseppe Verdi, was an ardent patriot who wanted the Austrians expelled from Italy, and he championed the cause of freedom in the rousing tunes of his early operas. He came from a humble peasant home, and his passionate nature was fired by dramatic stories. He has been criticised for choosing plots that are complicated and improbable, but he chose them because they involved strong characters and powerful emotions, and he was able to make audiences accept them by the sheer force of his music.

Il Trovatore, for example, is the absurd story of two brothers who don't know they are brothers (one was stolen when a baby by a mad gipsy) and who compete to the death for the love of the same woman. In the famous *Miserere* scene, the heroine sings outside the tower where her lover is imprisoned. She is interrupted by the sound of monks chanting the *Miserere* (a prayer for those about to die), and then she hears the voice of her lover singing farewell to her before he dies. The music is so exciting and dramatic that no one could ask themselves at this moment whether such a scene could ever really happen. The music expresses the truth of the characters' feelings, and we recognise that their anguish is artistically right.

In all his operas Verdi compels us to accept the inner

reality of such feelings as love, jealousy, greed, revenge, ambition, though he presents them in dramas that are now very remote from our lives. He, however, lived in a world in which prisoners and tyrants were very much a part of life – as in many places they still are – and he himself had narrowly escaped death as a child when his village was looted by Russian soldiers who killed many of the women and children.

His two greatest operas, *Othello* and *Falstaff*, were written at the end of his life, but it's easier to start with his early successes, *Rigoletto*, *Il Trovatore* and *La Traviata*. They are all tragic, deeply moving operas with wonderful tunes that will appeal to you straight away.

Verdi's grandest opera, *Aida*, is very expensive to stage, so if you do come across a production, don't miss it. It was written to celebrate the opening of the Suez Canal, takes place in Ancient Egypt, and needs the most splendid sets. Professor Swanston begins his book on opera by describing how his grandfather became an opera addict after seeing a performance of *Aida*. He never forgot the sight of the hero and heroine, having chosen to die together, being buried under a mound of sand – and nothing was ever so exciting again. This is the ideal way to discover opera.

The other towering figure of nineteenth-century opera, Richard Wagner, dedicated himself to it with a seriousness that in time was to revolutionise opera-going. He saw opera as the work of art of the future that would combine all the other arts, and as well as writing the music for his operas he also chose the stories, wrote the librettos, and supervised every detail of their staging down to scenery, costumes and lighting.

He was only able to do this because he was ruthless and utterly self-centred, but he believed that the artist has to override all opposition and use every means at his disposal, including flattery and dishonesty, in order to achieve his ideal. Wagner realised that he could only carry out his ideas in a theatre that had been specially built for his productions, and to achieve this he made use of the young King Ludwig II of Bavaria, who adored Wagner's operas and was delighted to spend money on them. Ludwig wanted the theatre to be built in his capital, Munich, but his courtiers intrigued against Wagner, whom they disliked, and it was some years before a suitable site was found at Bayreuth. The theatre was paid for by Wagner's friends and admirers (including the ever-generous Ludwig), and it finally opened in 1876 with the first performance of *The Ring*.

This story of the birth, love, betrayal and death of the great hero Siegfried took Wagner about twenty years to complete, and it stretched out into four closely-linked operas. They are full of excitement and drama, and the story rises to a mighty climax in which the heroine Brunnhilde builds a vast funeral pyre for Siegfried's body and then rides into the flames on his horse while the River Rhine, the source of the gold for the ring that has caused all the trouble, overflows its banks and sweeps over the pyre.

Instead of telling his story in the usual operatic way, Wagner discovered how to make the music itself explain and comment on what was happening. One of the ways in which he did this was by using themes (*leitmotiv*) to identify characters and ideas. These appear in all the four operas and signal what is important in a particular scene.

Nothing in the new theatre was allowed to distract attention from the stage – even the orchestra was out of sight. Wagner wanted his audience to submit completely to a great spiritual experience, and once the lights were lowered (even this was new) no latecomers were admitted and talking was firmly discouraged. Today we take these things for granted – and you should never arrive late or talk during music – but in Wagner's time such an attitude was revolutionary.

It was hard for any composer to follow such giants as

Verdi and Wagner, but one Italian who did make a great name for himself was Puccini. He had a wonderful gift for writing memorable and thrilling tunes, and a superb sense of popular theatre, and these qualities made Italian audiences in particular adore him. Today the gallery of La Scala is still packed with people who may not care much for other operas but know every note of Puccini's music and judge new stars by what they make of the great showpieces such as 'Che gelida manina', 'Vissi d'arte' and 'Nessun dorma'. Every opera-goer has probably seen *La Bohème* and *Tosca*, and you'll find them very easy to enjoy.

Sadly there isn't space to do more than mention some of the other important opera composers of this century: Richard Strauss, Alban Berg, Serge Prokofiev, Shostakovitch, Benjamin Britten, and Michael Tippett. Britten is the most successful British composer, and *Peter Grimes* and *Billy Budd* are now being revived and look like becoming operas that are put on regularly.

When you go to the opera, make sure that you arrive in time to read the outline of the plot in your programme. If you like opera, you may want to buy a book of *synopses*, so that you can get the plot quite clear in your mind before you start out. The best-known guide is Kobbe's *Complete Opera Book*, which tells you about more than 300 operas, but there are also some cheaper paperback guides.

But grasping the plot is only part of the problem. Most composers use librettos written in their own language, and English has never been one of the main languages of opera. For a long time Italian was the only language, but both French and German have impressed their sound on opera. And in some ways the sound can be as important as the meaning.

It may be frustrating not to understand what a singer is saying, but translation isn't always the cure. An

Italian singing Puccini in English would sound incongruous, and things that sound delightful in French or Italian may be rather ridiculous in English. Our associations with an English expression may conjure up quite the wrong picture when we hear it on the lips of a nobleman or a heroine in a highly emotional state.

Covent Garden keeps to the tradition of singing most operas in their original language, but the English National Opera has a more home-grown policy and puts on its operas in English. The best way of finding out which you prefer is to try both. You may find that most of the words are inaudible anyway, but I prefer 'Che gelida manina' to 'Your tiny hand is frozen' and feel it's worth the extra trouble of finding out the plot beforehand.

Although you may be moved by even a poor performance of a Beethoven symphony or a Mozart concerto, it's much harder to be carried away by a poor performance of an opera. So no wonder opera singers are treated like gods and goddesses. They are largely responsible for the success or failure of the evening, because no matter how good the sets are, how splendid the orchestra and the conductor, how spirited the chorus, the whole thing will remain earthbound if the stars won't or can't shine.

And there are few really great stars. They need a voice that is big enough to rise above the orchestra and dominate the music, a voice that sounds beautiful whether it is high or low, loud or soft, the ability to act, to move well and to look good on stage, and the kind of presence that can turn a stout tenor into a handsome young lover.

Oddly enough, although more training is available nowadays,it hasn't increased the number of great singers. A wonderful voice is a gift, and it's so rare that it has made the fortune of anyone so blessed, from the famous Italian tenor Enrico Caruso, who rose from the back streets of Naples to become one of the greatest singers in the world, to his modern counterpart, Luciano Pavarotti.

The word *primadonna,* which means literally *first lady,* has come to be associated with displays of temperament, and certainly some singers are as famous for their offstage scenes as others are for their vast size. The jokes about large ladies are well founded – Maria Callas was vast at one stage and Rita Hunter is no lightweight – and it may seem incredible that they should sometimes play heroines who are meant to be wasting away, like Mimi in *La Bohème.* There's no denying they can be a challenge to the imagination, but as with all the other improbabilities of opera, if the performance is great enough, one can be persuaded to accept any improbability.

10 Operettas and musicals

The idea of a play with music and dancing and extravagant settings was an attractive one, but something as grand as opera was not everyone's taste. As early as 1728, John Gay in *The Beggar's Opera* put together an entertainment that borrowed a certain amount from opera, including some of the best tunes, but was above all lighthearted and topical.

The story was about a highwayman called Macheath and his associates, and it made fun of some of the leading politicians of the day and laughed at the Italian operas that Handel had made so popular. It took London by storm; soon everyone was whistling the tunes, and in true musical comedy style the first actress to play Macheath's girlfriend later married a duke.

The Beggar's Opera was an English reaction to the seriousness of grand opera, but as we have seen, comic opera had become popular elsewhere and in time Paris and Vienna gave birth to lighthearted musical extravaganzas known as *operettas*. Vienna in the nineteenth century was a city of pleasure, and its charm, gaiety and elegance were mirrored in the enchanting music of the two Strausses, father and son.

Johann Strauss the Elder taught himself to play the violin and joined an orchestra when he was still a boy.

Later he formed his own orchestra, and they used to play in the Sperl, a popular beer-garden and dance-hall. They sat on a platform in the middle of the garden, and the customers were attracted by the stream of waltzes that flowed unending from Strauss's violin. It was music for dancing, and an intoxicating mixture of folk tunes and snatches from the latest operas and symphonies.

Strauss became so famous that he was invited to play all over Europe, and in 1838 he came to Britain for the celebrations in honour of Queen Victoria's coronation – and wrote a waltz to mark the occasion. Some of his waltzes are still played but he is chiefly remembered for his *Radetzky March*.

Oddly enough, in view of his success, he wasn't keen on his eldest son becoming a musician, and at first Johann the Younger had to take violin lessons in secret. Later he was able to study properly, and he soon formed his own orchestra and began to rival his father. In 1863 he was appointed director of the imperial court balls, and his music reflects the glitter and elegance of court life. Most of his great waltzes – *The Blue Danube, Roses from the South, Tales from the Vienna Woods* – date from this period, and it is easy to see why he was called 'The Waltz King'. He also wrote many other dances including the lively *Tritsch-Tratsch* and *Thunder and Lightning* polkas.

In 1863 Strauss met the French composer Offenbach, who was visiting Vienna, and Offenbach encouraged him to try his hand at writing an operetta. He was just as successful at this, though of the sixteen he wrote only two, *Die Fledermaus* (*The Bat*) and *The Gipsy Baron*, are still performed. As you would expect, they are full of good tunes and splendid waltzes.

Strauss's successor in Vienna was the Hungarian composer Franz Lehar, who began his career with a military band. His first operetta, *The Merry Widow*, was to be his most popular, and following true Strauss tradition it has an irresistible waltz.

If the Viennese operettas were dashing and romantic, the French operettas, particularly those of Offenbach, were sparkling and frivolous. Although a German, Offenbach went to Paris as a boy and spent the rest of his life there. He wrote nearly ninety operettas, but the only ones you are likely to hear and see today are *La Belle Hélène*, *Orpheus in the Underworld*, with its well-known Can-Can, and the mysterious and beautiful *Tales of Hoffman*, which has a haunting *barcarolle* or Venetian boating-song.

Offenbach used the old Greek legends to make fun of society, and the satirical possibilties of light opera also appealed to two Englishmen who formed one of the most brilliant and unlikely musical partnerships.

Gilbert and Sullivan were both successful in their own fields by the time they met. Sullivan's music had brought him fame at the age of twenty, and he had gone on to write drawing room ballads, hymn-tunes (the best-known is 'Onward Christian Soldiers'), cantatas and oratorios. He knew all the best people, from royalty downwards, had a glittering social life, and was the great hope of English music.

Gilbert had made his name as a writer. He wrote stories, criticism, a series of rather cruel verses called the *Bab Ballads*, and a large number of plays that did well at the time but have never been heard of since. Unlike the popular, easy-going Sullivan, Gilbert was a peppery man who spoke his mind, liked to get his own way, and was prepared to put up a fight to do so.

The two men were opposites, but they were brought together by a clever and farsighted theatrical manager, Richard D'Oyly Carte, who had a genius for spotting winners. He found the money to stage the operas and later built a theatre, the Savoy, specially for them. During the thirteen years of the partnership he was to spend a lot of time patching up quarrels, some of which he also helped to start.

The first great success came in 1878 with *H.M.S. Pinafore*, and it set a pattern that was to be followed in all the later productions. Gilbert thought up the story, wrote the dialogue and the words for the songs, and sent these to Sullivan, who then set them to music. It has been suggested that Gilbert's contribution was inferior to Sullivan's but this is not true. His libretto called forth Sullivan's music, which wouldn't have existed without it, and although each of them at times resented his dependence on the other, it was truly as Gilbert once called it a 'master and master' collaboration.

Sullivan would play his songs to the cast and conduct on the opening night, but it was Gilbert who brought the production to life. He had an exact idea of how each opera should be staged, and he was not prepared to allow any interference from the cast. He deliberately chose actors who were not well-known and were ready to accept his directions, and he made them into stars who were famous only as Gilbert and Sullivan players. Gilbert knew how he wanted every line of dialogue said, every song accented, he planned all the action and comic gestures – and his directions are still followed to this day by the D'Oyly Carte company. Such a regimented approach sounds a most unlikely recipe for success, but it worked.

Pinafore was to be typical of all the operas in its improbable plot, witty patter, songs, stirring choruses and sense of humour. Gilbert didn't really like music and hated grand opera, so he was happy to make fun of the more ridiculous plots of Italian romantic opera. He also enjoyed taking a dig at his fellow Victorians, with their love of sentiment, respectability and patriotism – though Gilbert shared these feelings himself. In *Pinafore* he included a caricature of the publisher W. H. Smith, who had been appointed First Lord of the Admiralty though he knew absolutely nothing about the navy. Much of Gilbert's satire is still as fresh as Sullivan's music, because he saw the basic ridiculousness of human behaviour, which hasn't changed. The songs in *The Gondoliers* making fun of equality, such as the one that ends,

> When everyone is somebodee,
> Then no one's anybody.

are, if anything, even more appropriate today.

But while Gilbert was pleased with the success of the operas, Sullivan was more divided. He was grateful for the money they brought in, but he longed for a more highbrow success. His one attempt at grand opera was a failure, and yet wherever he went he heard people whistling his tunes, as though to remind him that he was a popular rather than an artistic success.

But Sullivan misunderstood his genius. There is nothing second-rate about the string of delightful tunes that came to him as he worked away feverishly in the middle of the night and which he orchestrated with delicacy and sensitivity. The public rightly recognised *The Mikado* and *The Gondoliers* as his greatest triumphs, and were more reserved about *The Yeoman of the Guard*, in which he tried to be more serious.

Nearly a hundred years later the D'Oyly Carte productions still fill theatres, and the operas are the mainstay of amateur companies all over the world. They remain a unique record of a unique partnership, and they produced no imitations and no successors.

The European operettas travelled to America and in time gave rise to home-made imitations. Two of the most successful composers, Rudolf Friml and Sigmund Romberg, were born in Europe but made their names in New York with such shows as *Rose Marie, The Vagabond King, The Student Prince* and *The Desert Song*. They combined such popular ingredients as songs, dances, comedy, and spectacular scenes with a large chorus, but they haven't worn as well as Gilbert and Sullivan because people are no longer in sympathy with their romantic world of make-believe. Friml once said, 'I can't write music unless there are romance, glamour, and heroes' – and our idea of those has changed.

The American musicals of the 1920s and 1930s weren't about princes or poets in disguise, but they were just as far from real life. The plots followed the boy-meets-girl routine, and there were a lot of silly complications that had to be sorted out before the couple could live happily ever after. But audiences didn't mind. The words and music were so brilliant that no one worried about the improbability of the whole thing.

Few of the shows will ever be staged again, but you can get a good idea of their charm from the films of Fred Astaire and Ginger Rogers that are often shown on television. They are memorable for the unique talent of Astaire, whether dancing alone or with Ginger, and for the big production numbers with their lavish display of pretty girls and well-groomed men dancing with style and precision. It's impossible to stage such routines today, not only because they would be too costly but also because their carefree happiness isn't the spirit of our time.

But if the shows themselves haven't survived, many of their songs have. Songs such as Jerome Kern's 'Smoke Gets in Your Eyes', Irving Berlin's 'Cheek to Cheek', George Gershwin's 'I Got Rhythm' and Cole Porter's 'Night and Day' and 'I Get a Kick out of You' have gone on being arranged and adapted by singers, orchestras, groups and jazz musicians all over the world. They set a standard for popular music that has not been equalled since, and you can hear them sung at their best by such vocalists as Frank Sinatra and Ella Fitzgerald, who recorded a superb series of 'song books' of the greatest hits.

The songs are remarkable not only for their tunes but also for their witty and original words. Small revues gave young songwriters the chance to contribute one or two songs instead of having to write the whole show, and one team to benefit from this was Richard Rodgers and Lorenz Hart.

They met when Rodgers was sixteen and had already written a number of songs for amateur shows. He was much impressed by Hart, who was twenty-three, witty, cultured and sophisticated, and their partnership lasted for twenty-five years. They wrote about a thousand songs including 'Manhattan', 'My Heart Stood Still' (inspired by a near-accident in a taxi), 'The Lady is a Tramp', 'Blue Room', 'Mountain Greenery' and 'Bewitched'. The last two are good examples of Hart's brilliant lyrics, with their clever play on words and witty rhymes.

In the '20s and '30s two shows stood out from the silliness of the average musical and pointed the way to the future. The first was Jerome Kern's *Showboat*, in which the story, the characters, the setting and the music all combined to serve one another. Most of the action takes place on a boat on the Mississippi, which inspired the show's most famous song, 'Ol' Man River', and it deals with the problems of a girl who falls in love with a riverboat gambler, runs away with him, leaves him because of his gambling, and comes back to him years later, when their daughter becomes the new star of the showboat. Although the characters are cardboard, the plot corny and the ending too sweet, *Showboat* has lasted because of songs like 'Ol' Man River', 'Only Make Believe', 'Can't Help Lovin' Dat Man' and 'Bill', the touching account of love for 'just an ordinary man'.

The Negro problem hinted at in *Showboat* was to inspire George Gershwin's folk opera *Porgy and Bess*, which is more like an opera than a musical because all the dialogue is sung. Gershwin spent some time in South Carolina researching the background, and steeped himself in Negro music. The story is set in a Negro tenement and is a sad one. Bess falls in love with the crippled Porgy, who is kind to her when her boyfriend kills a man and goes into hiding. When he returns and upsets Bess, Porgy kills him and is taken off to prison. He is released because of the lack of evidence, but in the meantime Bess has gone to New York with another man. The opera ends with Porgy setting off on the long journey to find her.

Gershwin had raised musical comedy to the level of opera, and was criticised for it. Some people didn't like the sung dialogue, others such marvellous songs as 'Summertime', 'I Got Plenty of Nuttin' ', and 'It Ain't Necessarily So', which they said were too popular. Sadly Gershwin died before the opera was revived as a great success in 1942. He would have been thrilled that it was to be the first American opera ever put on at La Scala.

Musical comedy was growing up. It turned its attention to ordinary everyday characters. The 'heroes' no longer had to be pure upright men who weren't bright enough to do wrong, there were no out-and-out villains, and instead of having one or two funny characters, everyone shared in the comedy.

The first great break with tradition came in 1940 with Rodgers and Hart's *Pal Joey*. Joey (danced by Gene Kelly) was a weak unattractive man who was willing to give up the girl he loved in favour of a much older woman who was ready to buy him. In spite of some memorable songs, audiences didn't take to the show until it was put on again ten years later, but it made the point that in future musicals were going to be more realistic.

It was the last great Rodgers and Hart show – Hart died in 1943 – but Rodgers found himself a new partner in Oscar Hammerstein II. They embarked on a series of musicals – *Oklahoma!*, *Carousel*, *South Pacific*, *The King and*

I, The Sound of Music – that were to be the box-office and screen successes of all time. The settings varied from the American Midwest to New England, a Pacific island, Siam, the Austrian Tyrol, each adding a touch of local colour to the music, and they all had a string of memorable songs and a wholesome quality that made them ideal for all the family. Their records sold in millions, and all over the world their tunes were played as the accepted background to romance.

The 1940s and '50s saw other great successes too. There was Irving Berlin's noisy *Annie Get Your Gun*, with the large-voiced Ethel Merman triumphing as the liberated sharp-shooter who had to learn the hard way that you can't get a man with a gun, and the chorus hoisting the future national anthem of the entertainment world, 'There's no business like show business'. There was Cole Porter's *Kiss Me, Kate*, a lively version of Shakepeare's *The Taming of the Shrew*, Frank Loesser's offbeat view of Broadway life, *Guys and Dolls*, and after Lerner and Loewe's success with *Brigadoon* they turned Shaw's play *Pygmalion* into the brilliant *My Fair Lady*.

Rex Harrison gave an irresistible performance (on stage and screen) as the self-centred Professor Higgins, a selfish middle-aged bachelor who turns a flower girl into a duchess without realising that he has hurt her feelings. The lyrics softened Shaw's bite a little, and Cecil Beaton designed the most outrageous black and white costumes for the stunning scene at Ascot. The songs ranged from the exhilarating 'I Could Have Danced All Night' to the sentimental romance of 'On the Street where You Live' and cheery Cockney songs such as 'With a Little Bit of Luck' and 'Get me to the Church on Time'.

A more realistic and chilling note was struck by Leonard Bernstein's *West Side Story*, in which Romeo and Juliet were transported to the ugly world of gang warfare in Manhattan. The balcony scene became a duet on the fire-escape of a Puerto Rican tenement, and the antagonism between the teenage gangs, the Jets and the Sharks, was danced out in exciting savage routines arranged by Jerome Robbins who, like Bernstein himself, worked also in the world of serious music.

The British have not been able to match the large-scale technicolour talent of the Americans, but the songs of Noel Coward and Ivor Novello are assured of a place in light music. Coward wrote smart revues and romantic musical comedies such as *Bitter Sweet*, and his dry clipped voice remains the best interpreter of such witty songs as 'Mad Dogs and Englishmen' and 'The Stately Homes of England'. Novello had a gift for meltingly romantic songs such as 'We'll gather lilacs', and *The Dancing Years, Perchance to Dream* and *King's Rhapsody* delighted audiences who wanted to be taken back to the world of Ruritania, where dreams really do come true.

Vivian Ellis and Julian Slade both wrote charming carefree musicals, but Lionel Bart introduced a robust, more earthy note in his *Fings Ain't Wot They Used To Be* and *Oliver*, which was based on the familiar Dickens story.

In the 1960s, the big American successes – *Hello, Dolly, Fiddler on the Roof, Cabaret* – came and went, but the biggest impact was made by the rock musical *Hair*, which shook audiences not only with the sheer volume of the music but with a first-act finale in which all the cast were nude. The characters were dropouts, hippies who were against the draft and the war in Vietnam, and the big hit of the show, 'Aquarius', did seem to have brought in a new age.

But rock had no influence on the next new composer from America, Stephen Sondheim, whose shows *A Funny Thing Happened on the Way to the Forum, Company* and *A Little Night Music* pleased adult audiences rather than the young. Rock then teamed up with religion in *Godspell* and the even more successful *Jesus Christ Super-*

star, and the formula answered the need for a more dynamic approach to religion, for the ideals of the old world presented in the musical language of the young.

The glamour and glitter that had been such an important part of the musicals staged at Drury Lane were swept away by *A Chorus Line*, which did away with the big star, elaborate sets and costumes, and even the interval. And the confessions of the dancers who were auditioning for a place in the chorus line didn't pull any punches. They dwelt on failure and inadequacy, on the fear of not making good, and audiences seemed ready to enjoy such a complete reversal of escapism. But for how long? I suspect that the longing for romance and a world that offers scope for daydreams isn't banished that easily.

The exciting talents of Andrew Lloyd Webber and Tim Rice dominate the musical scene at the moment. The success of *Evita*, the story of the once powerful first lady of Argentina, has shown that *Jesus Christ Superstar* wasn't just a fluke, so perhaps the future of the musical will now be on this side of the Atlantic. You may be even more familiar with the pair's hit for children, *Joseph and the Amazing Technicolour Dreamcoat*, which many schools have performed.

11 Where to hear music

Once you become interested in music and start looking out for concerts, opera and ballet performances, recitals, lectures and workshop activities, you'll be surprised how much is going on all over Britain – far more than there is space to mention here.

I have concentrated on some of the most famous places and events not because they are always the best, but because they will be useful, I hope, to most people. So if your area isn't mentioned, this doesn't mean that you're living in a musical desert, but that it's up to you to do your own research. One of the best places to start is in your local library, especially if it has a music or record section, and other likely places for concerts are schools, colleges, churches and theatres.

If you haven't heard much music yet, or have been put off by the over-serious atmosphere of the one or two concerts you've been to, you might like to try one of the very special children's concerts staged by Atarah Ben-Tovim.

She's a dynamic blonde who used to be the principal flautist of the Royal Liverpool Philharmonic Orchestra until she decided to set up her own group, Atarah's Band, to put on musical entertainments that are designed to be fun. Her concerts are a cross between a circus, a symphony orchestra, a pop group and a pantomime, and she plays all kinds of music, from the classics to folk, jazz, rock and pop. The Family Proms include music from round the world and music used – and abused – on television (did you know that Dvorak likes his bread brown and Tchaikovsky sells chocolate?), and you also get the chance to take part in musical quizzes and rhythm games.

Atarah's Band gives concerts in schools and community centres as well as in places as far apart as the Usher Hall, Edinburgh, the Brangwyn Hall, Swansea, and the Wembley Conference Centre in London, but be sure to book well in advance, as the concerts are always a sell-out.

As well as putting on concerts and appearing on radio and television, Atarah Ben-Tovim also runs a Children's Concert Centre at Rossendale in Lancashire. Her Magic Music House has a library, rooms for practice and recitals, a Rock studio and a recording studio. You can get advice here on finding the right instrument for you, and if you are already learning an instrument, there are special master classes run by leading musicians. If you would like to know more about this, write to The Secretary, Children's Concert Centre, Regent Street, Haslingden, Rossendale, Lancs.

Concert-going can be an expensive hobby, so you may be interested in joining an organisation that gives music-lovers under twenty-five reductions of up to fifty per cent on tickets for a wide range of musical activities. In London, for example, they include performances at Covent Garden, the Coliseum, the Festival Hall, the Albert Hall, the Roundhouse, Sadler's Wells, the Fairfield Halls and the Wembley Conference Centre, and the scheme also operates all over the country.

Youth & Music prefers you to join as part of a group, but if this isn't possible, you can be an individual member. You'll receive a newsletter with details of all the events on offer, and Youth & Music also organises special recitals by young musicians and talks by such entertaining characters as percussionist James Blades, billed as 'the man who recorded the gong strokes for Rank films'. Youth & Music Yorkshire provides free coach travel from Bradford, Leeds and Sheffield to opera and ballet performances in London, so as you can see it really has a lot to offer. You can find out more, and how to join, from your school, or by writing direct to Youth & Music, 22 Blomfield Street, London EC2M 7AP.

London has become one of the great music centres of the world, and pride of place in the concert-stakes must go to the very modern complex of halls on the South Bank. The Royal Festival Hall, which opened in 1951, was built to celebrate an exhibition called the Festival of Britain. It's the first choice of all the great visiting orchestras and international soloists, and there's stiff competition among the top London orchestras to play here. One of the pleasures of going to a concert here – apart from the superb acoustics – is the wonderful view of the Thames from the great picture windows. It looks quite magical at dusk and a fitting scene for a capital city.

The Festival Hall is the scene of the Robert Mayer Concerts, which are held on Saturday mornings and also broadcast. As long ago as 1923, Sir Robert Mayer – who celebrated his hundredth birthday in 1979 – had the idea of special children's concerts at which the conductor could talk about the music and introduce the musicians. You can buy a season ticket for all six concerts, which include music by composers as varied as Telemann, Prokofiev, Dukas, Mozart and Stravinsky, and you'll find each item is introduced in a lively informative way.

The two smaller halls, the Queen Elizabeth and the Purcell Room, were opened in 1967 and are designed for smaller orchestras, chamber music and recitals. If you want to know what's going on here, for a small sum the

Box Office will send you a monthly calendar listing the concerts at all three halls.

The Albert Hall illustrates at a glance the difference between Victorian taste and ours. It's grand and ornate, with the scarlet and gold brilliance of an opera house, and an impressive dome that was the despair of musicians until a way was found of coping with the echo. It has a more warm-hearted atmosphere than the rather austere Festival Hall, and makes a splendid setting for large-scale choral works in particular.

But the most popular event of the year is undoubtedly the Proms, which in 1979 celebrated their eighty-fifth season. They moved to the Albert Hall when the Queen's Hall was bombed in 1941. and Sir Henry Wood's part in starting them is honoured in their name and by the bust of him that always gets a place on the platform and a wreath from the Young Promenaders.

Sir Malcolm Sargent was the chief conductor of the Proms for years, and he particularly enjoyed the antics of the Last Night, which traditionally include a rousing chorus of 'Land of Hope and Glory' by the whole audience, complete with Union Jacks, and further displays of patriotism in 'Rule Britannia' and 'Jerusalem'. Another tradition is drowning the orchestra in the hornpipe of the *Fantasia on British Sea Songs*, which somehow they manage to play faster than any audience can clap. It may look rather childish on TV, but it does express the high spirits of audiences who have been listening rapturously to music every night for nearly two months.

The burden of nightly concerts falls most heavily on the BBC Symphony Orchestra – the concerts are presented by the BBC and broadcast every night – but in 1978 orchestral guests included the four top London orchestras, the Hallé, the Bournemouth Symphony, the English Chamber Orchestra, the London Sinfonietta, the Monteverdi Orchestra, the Northern Sinfonia, and the BBC

Northern, Welsh and Scottish Symphony Orchestras. So if you'd had a season ticket, you could have seen and heard some of the best orchestras in the country. Two very exciting guests were the Chicago Symphony Orchestra and the Jeunesses Musicales World Orchestra, made up of young musicians from forty countries.

The Proms used to offer a crash course in the great accepted masterpieces, but in recent years they've become more experimental. Friday night is no longer automatically 'Beethoven Night', but now includes such composers as Janáček, Hindemith, Stravinsky, Lennox Berkeley and Schoenberg. In 1978, Beethoven's *Fifth* and *Seventh* symphonies were given a miss, and so were Bach's *Brandenburg Concertos*, but Handel just scraped in with the *Water Music*, played of course on old instruments.

You can buy an ordinary seat at the Proms, but it's cheaper and more fun to prom. This means joining a long queue outside and then going in the arena, where you look up at the orchestra and can just about see them when everyone's collapsed on to the floor, or right up to the top, where you can look down on everyone. The original idea of proms was that people were free to walk or 'promenade', about, but you won't find this too popular at the Albert Hall.

At the other end of the scale, the Wigmore Hall, which opened in 1901, specialises in chamber music and solo recitals. Many young musicians make their professional debut here, but you can also hear such great artists as Artur Rubenstein.

London also offers many more concerts in all sorts of settings, and it's worth keeping a special eye open for some of the more unusual. Open-air concerts are one of the pleasures of summer, when we get one, and my favourite takes place at the Crystal Palace and ends with a performance of Tchaikovsky's *1812 Overture* complete with cannon, fireworks, and flares that light up the trees as though they were being fired by an advancing army.

London doesn't have all the best orchestras, and the Free Trade Hall, Manchester, is the home of the Hallé, which has been giving concerts for over a hundred and twenty years. Its present conductor is James Loughran, but the orchestra also invites guest conductors and an impressive array of international soloists such as Alfred Brendel, Kyung Wha Chung, Stephen Bishop-Kovacevich, John Lill, Murray Perahia and Dame Janet Baker.

You can also see the Hallé in Bradford, Harrogate, Leicester and Sheffield, and it regularly tours Scotland, Wales and the South of England. It gives special School Concerts and has its own summer Proms. Other fine orchestras to be seen on tour as well as in their home towns are the Royal Liverpool Philharmonic, the City of Birmingham Symphony Orchestra, and the Bournemouth Symphony Orchestra.

The Welsh Arts Council runs a season of orchestral concerts in Wales featuring the BBC Welsh Symphony and the Welsh Philharmonic Orchestra plus visiting orchestras. They are a little limited by the lack of suitable buildings to house concerts, but a fine new National Concert Hall is being built at Cardiff. You can find out about the programme from the Welsh Arts Council, Museum Place, Cardiff – and you can get ticket concessions through Youth & Music (Wales).

Concerts in Scotland are listed in *Rostrum*, a monthly calendar available from the Scottish Arts Council, 19 Charlotte Square, Edinburgh. The Scottish National Orchestra give children's concerts and have a season of Proms in Dundee, Glasgow and Edinburgh, and like the two smaller orchestras, the Scottish Chamber Orchestra and the Scottish Baroque Ensemble, they appear in many parts of Scotland. If you're at school in the Grampian, Tayside, Fife, Central, Lothian and Strathclyde regions, you can get a sixty per cent discount on SNO concerts through the School Voucher Scheme, and parties of ten or more can get help with travel expenses. *Rostrum* also gives details of the many interesting events put on by local music societies all over Scotland.

Covent Garden is one of the great opera houses of the world and presents operas starring the leading international singers and conductors of the day and performances by The Royal Ballet. Tickets are expensive and not easy to get, but a small number of the cheapest (in the very back rows) are sold on the day, though you need to get there early (between 8.30 and 10 a.m.) and be prepared to queue until the box office opens at 10 a.m. Youth & Music offers reductions for one or two performances, and there's a short Prom Season in the spring with cheap places on sale an hour before curtain up.

If you prefer operas in English, make for the English National Opera at the London Coliseum, which puts on most of its productions in English and encourages British singers. The success of this policy led it to start a new company, English National Opera North, in 1978, and this is based in Leeds. The London company takes its productions on tour (while the Coliseum is filled by visiting ballet companies such as the superb Stuttgart Ballet), so you've a good chance of catching up with fine productions far away from London. Some seats for the Coliseum are always available on the day, and if you're really keen and fairly strong, you can also stand if the house is full. It's worth paying the small charge to be on the joint mailing list for Covent Garden and the Coliseum, which will keep you up to date on all opera and ballet performances.

This includes events at Sadler's Wells, the home of The Royal Ballet's main touring company, the Sadler's Wells Royal Ballet, who spend much of their time away from London. Sadler's Wells has a very interesting programme that includes appearances by the Ballet Rambert, the

London Contemporary Dance Theatre, Kent Opera, and the Handel Opera Society. All these companies can also be seen outside London.

Both the Scottish Ballet and the Scottish Opera have their home in Glasgow, but spend much of their time on tour. Scottish Opera makes a great effort to recruit new audiences through two offshoots, Scottish Opera for Youth and Opera Go Round. The first shows primary schoolchildren how to put on an opera themselves, and brings along costumes to share all the fun of dressing up. Opera Go Round stages economy performances, often with no more than five singers, a conductor and a piano, and also tours a special half hour show that may turn up at your school. The idea is to illustrate the bright tuneful aspects of opera through a made-up story that uses some of the best tunes. *Curtain Call*, one of their current shows, tells the story of a can-can dancer through the music of Offenbach. Secondary schools are also invited to provide the chorus for a specially commissioned rock opera, and are sent the music to learn beforehand. They then rehearse with the producer and principals before staging the show in public. For details of all their plans write to Scottish Opera, Elmbank Crescent, Glasgow.

Opera in Wales is provided by the Welsh National Opera, a fine company that regularly takes its productions on tour. To find out about their current programme and any special events for schools, write to them at John Street, Cardiff.

Today most towns seem to run some kind of arts festival, and music often gets pride of place. Many festivals give places outside the usual concert circuit the chance to hear distinguished soloists – most festivals manage to capture at least one important name – and the more adventurous may take the risk of performing rarely heard music. So they could give you the chance to hear a little-known opera, some unusual instruments, or concerts designed to introduce the music of a particular period, such as those given at the York Early Music Festival.

One of the most famous festivals takes place in Edinburgh every autumn. It is called an International Festival, and lives up to its name by attracting some of the finest orchestras, opera companies and soloists in the world. A rather different but just as impressive festival is held at Aldeburgh in Suffolk, which was the home of the composer Benjamin Britten. He once gave as his reasons for starting the festival, 'I belong at home in Aldeburgh. I have tried to bring music to it in the shape of our local festival; and all the music I write comes from it . . . my music now has its roots in where I live and work . . .'

At first the beautiful church at Orford was used for concerts, but then the Old Maltings – where malt for brewing used to be made – at Snape were converted into a superb concert-hall. If you live near, you may have been to a schools concert there. The festival likes to draw attention to composers who have been neglected or forgotten and to help living composers by commissioning new works, and of course it has always presented music by Britten. Many of his choral works have important parts for children's voices, and for one of the first festivals, back in 1949, he wrote a special children's opera, *The Little Sweep*, in which the audience too were asked to join in.

There isn't space to mention all the places that now have festivals – just listing them would take up several pages – but do find out what's going on in your area. You may get the chance to hear music in a historic building or some other very atmospheric setting, and this is certainly one of the advantages of church music and organ recitals.

Sunday is the obvious day for hearing the choir at its most magnificent – perhaps singing a beautiful setting of the mass at choral communion – but most cathedrals and some Oxford and Cambridge colleges also sing evensong every afternoon during term time. The service is held around four o'clock, and the musical showpiece will probably be the anthem, a short piece that will really test the choir. Anybody is welcome at this service, and you can take part simply by enjoying the music.

It's worth trying to afford live music as often as possible, but you'll also want to buy records of your favourite music so that you can get to know it really well. It's a temptation to go for the bargain issues and for the famous names, but this may not mean that you get the best recording.

Finding out what *is* best isn't too difficult. New recordings are reviewed every month in a magazine called *Gramophone* (which you'll find in your library), and if you don't want to be as specialist as this, they also publish a little booklet called *Recommended Recordings* that comes out twice a year and tells you the best records to go for if you want to build up a good classical collection.

You might also like to consult *The Gramophone Guide to Classical Composers & Recordings*, which gives you the lives of more than 130 composers and details of the best recordings of their works, and the various record guides published by Penguin Books. They will help you to find out the leading artists in every field, some of whom you may never have the chance to hear in person.

It's important, right from the beginning, to build up your standards from the best at an age when you can hear it most clearly and it will make the most impression upon you. Music is a pleasure that grows with you and always has new doors to open, and if you give it a chance, it will last you a lifetime.

We hope you have enjoyed this Beaver Book. Here are some of the other titles:

Enjoying Ballet A Beaver Original. Jean Richardson's survey of the history of ballet and today's best-known companies, performances and stars, illustrated with black and white photographs and with a foreword by Anthony Dowell of the Royal Ballet

The Beaver Book of the Seaside A Beaver original. Snorkelling and surfing, birdwatching and beachcombing – plus facts about ships, lighthouses, smuggling, wrecks, and lots of other fascinating topics. A book for everyone who loves the seaside by Jean Richardson; illustrated by Susan Neale and Peter Dennis

Conrad Mrs Bartolotti has the surprise of a lifetime when the postman delivers a tin can with a factory-made child inside. The ups and downs of life with the all-too-perfect Conrad and his scatterbrained mother are recounted by Christine Nostlinger in her hilarious book for readers of nine upwards. Illustrated by Franz Wittkamp

These and many other Beavers are available at your local bookshop or newsagent, or can be ordered direct from: Hamlyn Paperback Cash Sales, PO Box 11, Falmouth, Cornwall TR10 9EN. Send a cheque or postal order, made payable to The Hamlyn Publishing Group, for the price of the book plus postage at the following rates:

UK: 22p for the first book plus 10p a copy for each extra book ordered to a maximum of 92p;
BFPO and EIRE: 22p for the first book plus 10p a copy for the next 6 books and thereafter 4p a book;
OVERSEAS: 30p for the first book and 10p for each extra book.

New Beavers are published every month and if you would like the *Beaver Bulletin*, which gives a complete list of books and prices, including new titles, send a large stamped addressed envelope to:

Beaver Bulletin
The Hamlyn Group
Astronaut House
Feltham
Middlesex TW14 9AR

363538